Psychopaths in Our Lives

My Interviews

Dianne Emerson

FOREWORD BY CARL B. GACONO, PHD &
AARON J. KIVISTO, PHD

Psychopaths in Our Lives: My Interviews

© 2015 by Dianne Emerson

Edited by Katharine Worthington

CONTENTS

FOREWORD ....*v*

INTRODUCTION *1*

CHAPTER ONE *9*
    Comments about the Book

CHAPTER TWO *25*
    Nature or Nurture?
    Diagnosis, Childhood and
    Family

CHAPTER THREE *59*
    Self Image: Good versus Evil

CHAPTER FOUR *113*
    Gaslighting:
    Control through
    Manipulation

CHAPTER FIVE *175*
    Relationships

CHAPTER SIX *257*
    Psychopaths and Work

CHAPTER SEVEN *275*
    Eyes

AFTERWORD *287*

REFERENCES *293*

FOREWORD

By Carl B. Gacono, Ph.D. & Aaron J. Kivisto, Ph.D.

Perhaps no area of scientific study so naturally calls upon non-scientists to grapple with its most basic questions, as does the field of personality psychology. From the moment, we wake up to the time we go to sleep, we are typically inundated with stories of other peoples' behavior – whether it be loving, destructive, or anywhere in between. We learn *what* happened, *who* did what, *when* they did it, and *how* others responded. We get the facts. But, whether consciously or not, we all go beyond the information that we can so clearly see and hear.

The facts alone don't tell us what we seem to need to know. Each of us, sometimes deliberately and sometimes automatically, takes these facts and uses them as building blocks to infer motives for *why* others do what they do. We can't directly perceive these motivations through our five senses, yet we have a natural tendency to ascribe meaning to our experiences. To figure out the why for each what. Without an understanding of cause and effect, *why* others do what they do, our worlds feel like little more than a series of unintegrated and incoherent facts.

And so we all grapple with the basic questions faced by personality psychologists: why do people do what they do? And, given what this tells us about them, how might they act in the future? In fact, given just how naturally we seem to infer motives for others' behavior, one might feel sympathy for Dragnet Detective Joe Friday's uphill – and probably futile – battle to get his interviewees to stick to "just the facts, ma'am." This seems to violate our need to understand others, even when (especially when?) their behavior is cruel and appears incomprehensible.

What exactly *is* personality, and what does it mean when it's "disordered"? Broadly speaking, personality can be defined simply as the characteristic ways in which a person tends to perceive the world, think, feel, view themselves, and relate to others (Mayer, 2005). Further, contemporary understandings of personality recognize that these characteristics exist on a continuum rather than as discrete attributes that are either present or absent (Marcus, Lilienfeld, Edens, & Poythress, 2006). For example, we all fall somewhere along a range of agreeableness to disagreeableness rather than simply being agreeable or disagreeable. We're not introverted *or* extraverted, but somewhere between the two.

Given this, when is personality "disordered," or "disordered enough" to warrant a psychiatric diagnosis of a personality disorder? According to the American Psychiatric Association's *Diagnostic and Statistical Manual – 5th Edition* (DSM-5; APA, 2013), which distinguishes between 10 categories of personality disorders, a personality disorder is diagnosable when an individual's characteristic ways of thinking, acting, and relating to others (1) deviate markedly from cultural norms and (2) are exhibited across multiple contexts. Put another way, most peoples' behavior in a given situation reflects a relatively balanced combination of personality-based and situational causes. However, the personality-disordered individuals' behavior reflects a rigid imposition of their personality that is unresponsive to the unique demands of different situations and settings. When this rigidity impairs peoples' ability to function in work, love, and other important areas of their lives, they are considered to have a personality disorder.

It has also been suggested that a distinguishing feature between the personality disorders and other psychiatric diagnoses lies in the locus and scope of the suffering that the disorder entails. Most psychiatric disorders, such as Major Depressive Disorder, are diagnosed due to the suffering of the afflicted individual, as it is the exception rather than the rule that the individual with depression causes destruction and suffering in others' lives. Personality disorders, by contrast, are notable for the broad swath of suffering often experienced by others in the person's life, sometimes combined with little or no suffering in the individual diagnosed with the personality disorder.

With no diagnosis is this distinction more clear than with Antisocial Personality Disorder (ASPD). It would often be absurd to suggest that the diagnosed individual "suffers from" ASPD, although those who have had the misfortune of encountering such individuals will very often have suffered in some way. Why do people with ASPD – and its more severe variant, psychopathy – create so much destruction? To begin to answer these questions, it's essential to explain how psychologists recognize and diagnose these individuals.

Despite the fact that the antisocial syndromes, particularly psychopathy, have been the focus of more research than any other personality disorder, terms such as sociopathy, Antisocial Personality Disorder, and psychopathy are often misused and inaccurately viewed as synonymous (Losel, 1998; Gacono, 2000, 2015; Gacono & Meloy, 1994). Conflating these terms ignores the empirically distinct and clinically relevant differences of these constructs, which developed along separate theoretical lines. Psychopathy originated with Pinel's (1806) clinical observations and introduction of the term *manie sans delire*, or madness in the absence of delirium. The idea that there existed a type of madness that could spare central mental functions was considered revolutionary at the time, but largely went nowhere for the next hundred years. In 1907, Emil Kraeplin, the father of psychiatric nosology, introduced the term "psychopathic personality," although his clinical observations about these difficult patients failed to gain momentum.

Eventually, however, Hervey Cleckley's groundbreaking 1941 text, *The Mask of Sanity*, established psychopathy as a valid topic of scientific study and introduced a model of psychopathy that remains central to contemporary understandings. Key to Cleckley's model of psychopathy was the dual emphasis on both behavioral and trait criteria. Cleckley (1941/1976), in contrast to Pinel's emphasis on focal cognitive and affective defects, framed psychopathy in terms of the personal suffering and social costs psychopaths continually inflict on others. Psychopaths, according to Cleckley, were epitomized by a combination of 16 (reduced from

21 in the original text) characteristics that are associated with an impulsive, irresponsible, and deceitful life-style. In psychoanalytic parlance, the psychopath was pathologically devoid of conflict about the causes or consequences of his antisocial acts. The psychopath's urge to take, break, or hurt were seen as never truly proportionate to the objects of their efforts, and Cleckley (1941/1976) observed that their antisocial acts often appeared surprisingly lacking in external motivation. The psychopath either blithely ignored reality or refused to acknowledge it. To Cleckley's psychopath, taking, breaking, and hurting were goals in their own right, with each antisocial act bolstering the individual's profound egocentrism.

Shepherding Cleckley's (1941) model of psychopathy into contemporary clinical and forensic practice, Robert Hare developed the Psychopathy Checklists (Hare, 1991, 2003; Forth, Kosson, & Hare, 2003; Hart, Cox, & Hare, 1995), which have become the gold standard for evaluating psychopathy (Gacono, 2000, 2015.) Mirroring Cleckley's emphasis on both trait and behavioral aspects of psychopathy, the Psychopathy Checklists contain two stable factors. The first factor, "callous, remorseless use of others" (Factor 1), is characterized by egocentricity, callousness, and remorselessness, and correlates with Narcissistic and Histrionic Personality Disorders, low anxiety, low empathy, and self-report measures of Machiavellianism and narcissism (Hare, 2003). The second factor, "antisocial lifestyle" (Factor 2), represents an irresponsible, impulsive, thrill-seeking, unconventional, and antisocial lifestyle and correlates most strongly with criminal behaviors, lower socioeconomic background, lower IQ, less education, self-report measures of antisocial behavior, and the diagnoses of Conduct Disorder and Antisocial Personality (Hare, 1991, 2003).

In contrast to psychopathy, sociopathy (APA, 1952) and Antisocial Personality Disorder (APA, 1994, 2013) are terms that have evolved across various editions of the American Psychiatric Association's *Diagnostic and Statistical Manual of Mental Disorders* (DSM).

The term sociopathy, which lacks contemporary clinical meaning, was introduced by Birnbaum in 1909 to describe individuals exhibiting antisocial behavior, impulsivity, and deficits in empathy and emotional processing. In contrast to conceptualizations of psychopathy at the time, which tended to emphasize a hereditary etiology, sociopathy emphasized the role of environmental factors and personal experiences. A pathological social context was both the cause and consequence of the sociopathic individual's behavior.

In the first edition of the DSM, which was introduced in 1952, Birnbaum's notion of sociopathy was included as a diagnosis of "sociopathic personality disturbance." In the 1968 edition of DSM-II, however, the term sociopathy was replaced by Antisocial Personality Disorder (ASPD). ASPD was defined by its emphasis on incorrigible antisocial traits and behaviors, such as egocentrism, callousness, impulsivity, guiltlessness, and recalcitrance to remediation efforts or punishment (APA, 1968). To the extent that the definition of ASPD in DSM-II (1968) still captured both observable behaviors as well as personality traits, it was in some ways still quite consistent with Cleckley's (1941) model of psychopathy.

The DSM-III ASPD criteria largely jettisoned the trait features of ASPD and focused primarily on observable behavior (APA, 1980), based largely on the work of Lee Robins (1966), the increasing popularity of a social deviancy model in psychiatric circles, and the aim of increasing inter-rater reliability. The nearly exclusive focus on observable traits has continued through the current DSM-5 criteria for ASPD (APA, 2013). However, what was sacrificed in the interests of increasing reliability was the usefulness (validity) of the disorder (Gacono & Meloy, 1994).

Today, ASPD is most accurately viewed as a diagnosis rooted primarily in socially deviant behavior, regardless of the personality traits of the individual engaged in deviant conduct, whereas psychopathy captures both the problematic behavior as well as the traits that presumably facilitate such misconduct.

There are several implications of psychopathy's two-factor structure versus the single factor associated with ASPD. First, whereas one can arrive at the ASPD diagnosis by a virtually unlimited number of criteria combinations,[1] categorizing vastly different individuals under the

---

[1] The possible variations in ASPD diagnoses for DSM-III and DSM-III-R combined at roughly 27 trillion; while the DSM-IV offers 3.2 million variations (Rogers, Salekin, Sewell, & Cruise, 2000). The CD (APA, 1994) diagnosis also encompasses a heterogeneous group of children and adolescents with community base rates estimated at 3% to 5% of school age children (male to female ratio = 4:1--9:1).

umbrella of this single diagnosis; psychopathy constitutes a more homogeneous syndrome. As a result, base rates for ASPD and psychopathy are significantly different. While ASPD community rates are estimated at 5.8 % of males and 1.2% of females, prison populations will typically have rates of 50% to 80%. Psychopaths will comprise only 15 to 25 percent of the same prison populations.

Finally, and probably most importantly, psychopathy assessment has important clinical and forensic implications in terms of predictive validity, (Gacono, Loving, & Bodholdt, 2001; Gacono 2000, 2015). For instance, high PCL or PCL-R scores have been associated in the research with a higher frequency and wider variety of offenses committed, higher frequency of violent offenses, and higher re-offense rates (Hare, 2003); poor treatment response (Ogloff, Wong, & Greenwood, 1990; Rice, Harris, & Cormier, 1992); and more serious and persistent institutional misbehavior (Gacono, Meloy, Sheppard, Speth, & Roske, 1995; Gacono, Meloy, Speth, & Roske, 1997; Heilbrun, et al., 1998). The ASPD diagnosis is not associated with these same outcomes (Lyon & Ogloff, 2000). One possible interpretation of the relative disconnect between the diagnosis of ASPD, and the prediction of future behavior is that the diagnosis, for all its inter-rater reliability, fails to facilitate understanding of the individual who has broken the rules.

Given the pull we all experience to understand not only *what* someone has done, but also *why* they did it, it is perhaps unsurprising that the antisocial syndromes have received so much attention. After the initial reactions of horror and fascination typically elicited by the acts of psychopathic individuals, the question most people struggle with is why. Contemporary clinical and forensic science has aided in this understanding, beginning with the work of Pinel in the early 1800s and solidified through Cleckley and Hare's enormous contributions. However, none of the contributions of these pioneers toward our understanding of psychopathic individuals would have been possible without the stories of the psychopaths that they encountered. It is easy to lose sight of the centrality of these stories, in large part because they are so rarely detailed.

In the pages that follow, Dianne Emerson provides readers with the rare opportunity to enter the personal lives of three male psychopaths through their own words. Through the careful organization of their everyday stories of *who, what, when* and *where*, Emerson ultimately provides the building blocks for readers to understand *why* these individuals do what they do. Without such stories, there is little hope for understanding.

INTRODUCTION

"To ignore evil is to become an accomplice to it."
—Martin Luther King

This book is not the prototypical analysis of incarcerated psychopaths. I am not a psychiatrist, nor an academic researcher. What I offer is a new perspective on diagnosed and self-identified psychopaths, using their own words to reveal the truth.

Most psychopaths are not in prison but live among us; virtually, anyone can be victimized, in one way or another, typically without realizing how or why it happened to them. Over the years, several books have been published from the victim's point of view, but what interested me were some concepts that no one seemed to be talking about in any detail.

One such concept you will read about is gaslighting, an important tool psychopaths use to control their victims. The term is derived from the 1944 film, "Gaslight." In the movie, Paula (Ingrid Bergman) marries the evil Gregory Anton (Charles Boyer), not knowing that he murdered her aunt and is now trying to find her aunt's jewels.

To prevent Paula from finding out what he is doing, he makes her think she is going crazy. He moves things and tells her she put them there; he hides his watch and tells her she stole it; finally, he tampers with the gaslights, so they flicker, and told her it looks fine to him.

He isolates her and prevents her from leaving the house, all to allow him to search the attic for the jewels without her realizing what he is doing. This is a type of manipulation, intended to make the victims doubt their own memory and sanity. I wanted to know how psychopaths viewed what they were doing.

I decided that perhaps the answers to my questions might come from the psychopaths themselves, so I embarked on a mission to identify and interview a few. I had operated an online discussion forum for over eighteen years to allow victims of psychopaths to connect, communicate, and share experiences.

Not surprisingly, it attracted the attention of a few psychopaths, some from a desire to learn about themselves, some from mere curiosity, and some who wanted to advise the victims.

Three of these men, whom I identify as "Fred," "Steve," and "Bill," carried on extensive email conversations with me. They agreed to let me present their words in this book. I had some ground rules, such as all communications had to be in writing. I wanted to remove my emotions from the equation.

Psychopaths are experts at reading people, and I felt that with written text, I might come closer to the truth of their actions.

The conversations presented in this book give insight into the thoughts of these three men. Rather than present the conversations chronologically as they occurred, I have combined their comments by subject. Each chapter contains questions and answers from all three that pertain to a topic of discussion. In the end, I had hundreds of pages of communication. All the interviews presented are the actual dialogue.

Nothing was changed except for a few commas and typos here and there. I did not want any editing of their words because how they speak about things is often as interesting as what they are saying.

Although I present these as interviews with psychopaths, you will note that the interviewees sometimes use the term "sociopath" to describe themselves.

They seemed to view this term as less disparaging than psychopath, although at least one of them, Bill, is proud of being a psychopath and considers sociopaths to be at a lesser level. He compares himself to a lion, and sociopaths to hyenas.

You will notice their startling lack of compassion for their victims.

Bill commented about not understanding why victims are upset:

> "Even the gazelle in the Serengeti knows there are predators at every turn. Do you think when one is taken by a lion the others are dumbstruck "Oh my, I had no idea there were animals that would eat me." Absolutely not.

So why must humans seem so astounded when they have been taken advantage of? Why is this surprising?"

An interesting article in Scientific American said,

"In contrast to people with psychotic disorders, such as schizophrenia, who often lose contact with reality, psychopaths are almost always rational.

They are well aware that their ill-advised or illegal actions are wrong in the eyes of society but shrug off these concerns with startling nonchalance."[2]

Psychopaths use a combination of charisma, manipulation, coercion, and sometimes violence to control others and satisfy their own egocentric desires.

Psychopaths tend to be persuasive, charming, egotistical, impulsive, and risk seeking. They lack empathy; they lie; they do not accept responsibility for their behavior, nor do they show guilt or remorse to people they hurt. Their lack of a conscience is a distinguishing characteristic.

An article in the *Journal of Forensic Psychiatry and Psychology*[3] commented that psychopaths appear to enjoy what they do; they have no fear of

---

[2] Lilienfeld, S.O. & Arkowitz, H. (2007). What "psychopath" means: It is not quite what you may think. *Scientific American*.

[3] Rogers, T., Blackwood, N., Farnham, F., Pickup, G., Watts, M. (2008). Fitness to plead and competence to stand trial: A systematic review of the construct and its application.

punishment, and they are not disturbed by social stigmatization.

The conversations you will read suggest that they are concerned about being caught. When I asked Fred about his opinion of using drugs to control someone, his response was,

"That's really pretty deplorable. It's also profoundly stupid, because it is leaving a chemical trail that will be picked up if the person goes into meltdown and ends up seeking medical attention. "Why do I feel like this?" being answered with "because according to your blood reports you keep eating contraindicated mood meds" is going to fairly quickly lead back home."

Fred was less worried about the ethical aspect of drugging someone than about the risk to himself.

Common thinking is that psychopaths are unconcerned about the expectations of society and ignore its judgment of their behavior. This is true to an extent: any effort they make to fit into society's norms is part of their mask. Bill said,

> "The person you need me to be in order to trust, confide in, support and promote is the person I will become.
>
> Being free of unpredictable emotional reactions and guilt, I am free to be whatever, whenever and then change that when necessary."

Because of this mask, victims of psychopaths need help to recognize them and understand their thought processes. I hope to help them with my discussion forum and with this book.

How does one recognize a psychopath? There are clues, some subtle and some obvious. As you read this book, pay attention to the way these men talk about themselves and others.

The victims who post messages on my online discussion forum talk about fearing an outburst of anger, sometimes over nothing at all. They are afraid to deviate from a routine. Psychopaths need to have control, and tend to isolate their partners from family and friends.

They demand to know everything you do, everywhere you go, and may even spy on you or listen to your phone calls. It's all about control.

Psychopaths can be charming, and then turn on you suddenly. Typically, they have had a history of bad relationships. They will disparage their previous relationships.

Everything is always someone else's fault, whether in a relationship or at work.

Psychopaths will consistently blame another and portray themselves as the victims. Indeed victimizing others while shouting they are the victim.

Psychopaths have enormous egos. While not every narcissist is a psychopath, all psychopaths have narcissistic personalities. Their world revolves around themselves, and they are entitled to whatever they can get.

If someone crosses them, they will retaliate. If you dare to do something, they don't want they will be furious. They may scream at you, curse you, or even hit you. If they apologize afterwards, it is only to prevent you from leaving. They lie. They do not care about you.

On the other side, they might not show any reaction but plot behind your back to seek revenge. They will always find a way to even the score, whether directly or indirectly.

Some of what you read in this book will horrify you. It certainly horrified me. Some of it may sound frighteningly familiar. You will have a glimpse into the mind of the everyday psychopath, the one for whom you may work, the one whom you may run into in the grocery store or at the gym, or possibly the one with whom you live.

It would be nearly impossible to make it through life without encountering a few psychopaths on your journey.

CHAPTER ONE
Comments about the Book

"Any fool may write a most valuable book by chance, if he will only tell us what he heard and saw, with veracity."
—Thomas Gray, Letter to Horace Walpole

Dianne
I plan to incorporate our conversations into a book, so people can see what goes on in the mind of a psychopath that they might meet in business or socially. Do you have any thoughts about this, or problems with my including our discussions?

I am writing a book so that people will understand how you operate. I think it is clearly a win-win for both of us. I get to put the words to what all others before me have only tried to "describe.

Might I be teaching you how to operate better? I don't feel uneasy about that because I am looking at the larger picture.

Perhaps, but I understand that is our trade off. To get information from a higher lever psychopath, that has to be part of the bargain or no one with any real information would agree to be interviewed. I also feel like people can trust me because I have had an online discussion forum for almost eighteen years, which was the first one on this subject, and I have ZERO to gain by hunting anyone down. I have my own contacts in the industry and wouldn't need the help of the FBI to track anyone down.

I am very clear in what I am doing and won't cross any lines. I will keep your personal information and location between us. No one but myself will ever have your contact information. I will change your name, but I really doubt you have given me your real name in any case.

Bill
The publication of your book is something I look forward to. I am hoping you are including these interviews as they are what will actually demonstrate the thought patterns of the psychopath.

 will also demonstrates that we are not all the ones hiding in your closet, waiting for you to sleep, to remove your head and wear your skin as a dress.

I have no concern of you hunting me down. There would be nothing to gain by it. Unless, you are harboring a personal vendetta against any and all psychopaths. Which, frankly, does not really concern me.

I have not admitted to any criminal activity, nor will I, and simply being a psychopath has not yet been criminalized.

The FBI would have nothing to prosecute. Additionally, if you are attempting to write a series of books, it wouldn't bode well to lock up your interview subjects. I doubt you would get many more volunteers after that.

Steve
I would like a copy of the book when it comes out and feel free to spell check away writing has never been a strong point for me. But I would not like my name mentioned as it would complicate things in my life.

Dianne
Naturally, I will be glad to send you a copy when it is published. I think you will find it interesting. I hope it will provide new and interesting information to the readers, as this approach is unique for a subject that has not had sufficient attention. We all share the same earth so we should learn and understand more about each other.

Fred
If you would like me to answer any questions, I may be able to give insight on, then I am willing to answer and will understand if questions are kept brief and to the point, to avoid engagement.

I believe it would be possible to exchange mutually beneficial information based on fail-safe's (limited/non-engaged exchanges on a Q&A format, no requirement to provide me with any information, etc.) to assure you I mean you no harm.

I've no idea how many other people may have contacted you along similar lines (it seems likely some at least have or will, since we share the same interests), but it is likely I am one of the lower risk of those that may have. Since I have noticed something already, I can only assume any others would; you should probably disconnect this email account from your Facebook profile. I do not use the service, in case you were wondering. If I did and/or had any interest in using it, I would have been unlikely to tell you.

Am I a danger to you? In all honesty, I am not. That does not mean I consider "co-operation" something I would have an interest in (be capable of?) Perhaps, but I would need good reasons, and it would feel… "itchy", at least how I believe you understand the term.

I do not expect to win your trust in any meaningful sense, as you are clearly not so naïve as for it to be worth my time bothering.

Dianne
I think a person can find danger in a lot of places that don't always involve psychopaths. For example, the incidence of drivers impaired by alcohol is much higher late at night, and we all know that this group of people kills. Truckers that use methamphetamine are a danger on the road and can kill you.

People using heavy drugs like meth exhibit a clear lack of empathy and will rob you and then help you look for what is gone. Danger exists in lots of places.

Fred
Not that I think you are doing this, but tell me; are you consulting with anyone regarding our interaction? On how to act, what to watch for? Professional opinions on whether I am this? I mean other than me, of course. I do not mind if so. I ask because I have the impression you are. It's no problem

As to whether you would engage if you thought all sociopaths were bad to the core. I quite honestly do not know. Sometimes dirty jobs need doing, I guess.

Just it'd be easier in some ways for me if I could stop watching myself out of the corner of my eye constantly, but this isn't going to work if I do that and then fuck up by dropping the ball because neither of us was paying attention.

If I can trust you to not trust me, whilst also not just assuming everything, I say is a lie, then we don't end up in a situation we do not want, and we'll probably both get a much clearer picture. What do you think?

Dianne
I like it when people talk about themselves. I knew when we first started our conversation that this was all more about you than it ever would be about me. I like

being a good observer and listen well when others talk.

Alas, I don't have anyone helping me, do you think I should? Are there things that I am missing? For all you know I am catching and observing it all.

Perhaps I could call in a profiler like you see on crime shows that could sit by my side drinking coffee and give me scripts to write and questions to endlessly grill you with.

I prefer stream of conscious writing and will only bother with random spell checks, so I probably could use a good secretary more than anything.

Fred
I suggest that you lay out what areas you would be interested in conversing over, what you would expect to get out of such a conversation and what boundaries you feel would be appropriate. I can then say what of that I'm happy to agree to, and we can then work within this. Brevity is unlikely though, since these are complex matters and, well... the obvious reasons, really!

Dianne
To address the areas that I wish to cover, frankly, I believe in the free flow of information to see where things lead rather than limit the conversation to a set agenda.

In essence, the purpose of my writing is to clear up the image of what a psychopath is both in terminology and in how to deal with the differences between us in people's lives.

People go on the news and declare known killers as psychopaths when they cross a specific line, yet they seem to wither from identifying the head of a huge commercial enterprise that actually destroys more people than even the most prolific serial killer.

I do have a set of questions that I will ask everyone, but I am sure that as these interviews go along other questions will come to mind.

Fred
You mention what I may stand to gain from this, which is something I find increasingly difficult to guess at as to what you mean regarding, but I think you may be underestimating my curiosity and desire to learn.

You are unlikely to ever meet someone who is as interested in their boundaries and capacities as I am, nor someone as interested in those of others.

I have only two modes; scattered disinterest in the sense of casting an intellectual net in the hope of landing an interesting catch but with no direction or planning at all, or absolute laser-like focus that will tear apart the foundations of even my own sanity in order to find deeper understanding.

I think you may have the capacity to provide me with questions that I would not think to ask myself and enable me to find answers I would otherwise miss. In return, you would have some idea of how psychopath-type behaviors manifest internally and therefore, to better spot them.

Dianne
I hope you don't feel a need to censor yourself in any way to try to protect what you seem to be indicating might be my sensitive ears.

I am open to all view points and prefer to not have a filter to what I might or might not like, it would be hard for you to judge because perhaps I am different from others in your life that need the filter to protect the image you have created for them to enjoy?

I find all aspects of this topic of high interest, and short or long responses don't matter because it is the base of the information that interests me.

Fred
You have some interesting thoughts. I was wondering how you would interpret things written under the light of drama and grandiosity. I'm pleased to see you're not so easily caught up in it. This sometimes can be a big problem with people's misunderstanding of words.

I remember from university, there were several professors and many 'peers' who could study a book extensively – sometimes for years – and quote it verbatim, but had absolutely no idea what any of it meant.

That's what words can do to an untuned mind. If it sounds like nonsense at first and was written by someone who played the game well, it must be clever, right? Hah. Confused people read confused explanations and mistake familiarity for wisdom.

May I ask; what do you think other people could learn from our exchanges?

Dianne
I think a lot of people can learn from our conversations. I have been doing a couple of other smaller exchanges, mainly for a reference point. I know I find the human mind a fascinating subject. I think that is what I find so compelling about this particular subject.

Is a psychopath running a Ponzi[4] scheme, for example, seriously more to blame than all the people who mortgage his or her life savings to go along with a get-rich scheme?

---

[4] A Ponzi scheme is an investment scam promising high rates of return with little risk. It generates returns for earlier investors by acquiring new investors. It actually yields the promised returns to earlier investors, but only as long as there are new investors. These schemes collapse on themselves when new investments stop.

What level of greed is acceptable? Is the architect of the scheme a worse character than those are who choose to participate?

Perhaps if people understood more what drives psychopaths, they might think twice before falling for lures, they would be better off avoiding.

We are quick to blame, but perhaps we need to open our eyes and listen to our instincts. One observation made by every victim at my forum is that they brushed aside those red flags; I call it living life by painting those red flag's white.

Victims come in all shapes and colors. In general, the word victim is a broad term. What I am interested in is at what point we should take responsibility for getting into a situation that results in our being a victim.

Sometimes people become ensnared unsuspectingly, such as entering into a relationship with a psychopath; when it doesn't work out, at what point is the victim responsible?

In the opposite spectrum, if someone is murdered by a serial killer just because the killer is lurking around while they are walking to their car, they become a victim who has done nothing.

Fred

... Well, am I the one you want your book to be about or the one your book needs to be about? Articulate, educated, insightful, witty, quite startlingly modest and even sporting a deep, well-spoken British accent. But not vile.

Not beyond redemption (?). Not some violent brute, but not so sanitized that I'm just Joe Schmoe of Average Street. A psychopathic Goldilocks. One who isn't a monster, just a bit misunderstood and frightened, like everyone else.

Not that I'm mirroring that, as I'm trying to rigidly stay away from doing anything of the sort. I guess you could say that one day I'd like to look into a mirror and see me.

I hope there's not too much stuff that I'll feel needs to be altered at all, but where there is I am sure I can come up with minor changes that will make the whole thing unidentifiable enough for me not to worry. And I do worry about that, but shall not demand anything more than the absolute minimum required to resolve that.

Sorry to keep repeating this, but as I'm sure, you can understand. It is important to me. Going through all of this, staring myself in the eye and looking for my own soul, piecing together the fragments of mirrors... I do not want it all to be for nothing.

That means I want you to be able to use whatever segments you wish for your book, but I also want to be able to move on and find happiness and stability for myself. Otherwise, I may as well have killed myself a couple of months ago and saved myself the hardship. Does that make sense?

As I said, I do not know these matters as well as you do. However, in the name of intellectual integrity I felt the need to ask.

I do not want you to write a book based on false or misleading information. If I'm just some fruitcake who had a psychotic break, that would be a poor foundation for your book.

If I'm an increasingly self-aware sociopath, I do not want to undermine your book by dismissing myself as 'just some fruitcake' as part of a subconscious impetus towards a consciously-unknown goal. Trust, trust, trust. Do you trust me at all? Honest question.

Dianne
ardent I am not writing a slanted "all these people are bad" type of story. I want people to see the truth about what psychopaths are doing; I want people to recognize how they operate.

Fred
I did not mean to suggest that you have knowingly underestimated those things merely that I am not sure you can comprehend how powerful a drive it is. Life is about learning to be better at what we do, for all of us. Whether the person realizes it or not, every time they repeat an action they are learning to be better at what they do. This is a universal and necessary truism of human nature.

What am I hoping to learn to do better, do you think? What do I stand to gain here? You shall have a book - and probably a good one; I think - but I shall just have concerns about how my words are used. Although I suppose there is an irony to be appreciated there. But still, the questions stand.

I'm being as respectful, non-judgmental and honest as it is possible to be, but if you would rather I were not, then I shall bid you all the best with your book and humbly request that you take great measures to protect my identity, should you decide to use any of my reams of waffle.

Dianne
Thank you for participating. I would never be able to communicate the complexity of the mind of a psychopath without your valuable help.

As you probably know, most of what is written on this subject comes from the viewpoint of either the violent ones who hit the front page of newspapers or the ones identified by jilted lovers.

There has been a plethora of interviews with those imprisoned, but they are not anywhere as interesting as those who control their behavior.

In some cases, serial killers operate on a much lower intellectual level than psychopaths, who are successful in masking their true character.

Bill

The mask is also useful in personal relationships. If you were to look into my circle of "friends" you will see they all serve a purpose and change often. It is my understanding that this is the area your book focuses on. What, in particular, are you interesting in knowing?

I agree with your take, plan, for your book. This is one of the reasons I have an interest in maintaining this conversation.

I have read [Dr. Robert] Hare's books, and I am far from impressed. I would have expected a man with an academic background to provide more tangible stories opposed to his composites and fictions he provides in his books.

From his writings, it is obvious he has a bias against the psychopath, which I suppose it would be hard to find someone that doesn't.

Any intellectual reading these materials do not want to know what you think about psychopaths. They will want to know your experiences, your research and what lead you to such a conclusion. I would also suggest Hare's research is flawed, if not at least skewed.

He predominately interviews only prisoners. Men looking forward to participating in these research projects in an effort to look good to a parole board, or simply out of boredom.

The publication of your book is something I look forward to. I am hoping you are including these interviews as they are what will actually demonstrate the thought patterns of the psychopath.

CHAPTER TWO
Nature or Nurture?
Diagnosis, Childhood and Family

"There is no explanation for evil. It must be looked upon as a necessary part of the order of the universe. To ignore it is childish, to bewail it senseless."
— W. Somerset Maugham

Dianne
Have you had a chance to read my discussion forum and if so what would you like people to know to better understanding of your condition? Just to be clear the term psychotic indicates someone who can hear voices, etc.

The experts argue over whether the term psychopath or sociopath is best suited. I think most people feel like a sociopath is not going to hang out in alleys with a butcher knife, and they relate the term psychopath to serial killers like Ted Bundy[5].

Is that how you see the terms?

Fred
I have spent some hours reading your forum and can see your community helps people greatly.

---

[5] Ted Bundy was a serial killer, kidnapper, rapist, and necrophile who murdered numerous young women and girls during the 1970s. He confessed to 30 homicides committed in seven states between 1974 and 1978. The true victim count could be higher.

The damage that psychopathic behavior can cause, particularly in relationships, can be quite devastating and clearly, support and communication at your forum are very positive structures and outlets.

On the forum, I see many speculations on what is behind the so-called 'mask' of a psychopath. I believe I may be able to help answer this.

Dianne
Do you prefer the term psychopath or sociopath?

Steve
I prefer the term sociopath because I don't feel I am psychotic, just destructive. I found out I was like this was because I have had a number of relationship breakdowns, and they all ended the same way so if this was getting in the way of my plans,

I decided to see if it was me. It was two years ago now that I did the test for it, and well. It was me. And that is the main reason I prefer that name over the other one it's the link to violence that goes with it.

Fred
From what you have said already and what I have read, I would say I lay in the area more often called 'sociopathic'. This was something I was thinking about earlier, and I suspect that I may have started forming bonds when very young and then just

stopped. Do not ask what may have prompted this, because I do not know.

You also mention the sociopathy/psychopathy blur. If I am correct about myself, I would probably fit the common conception of the former slightly more neatly than the latter. I think the classifications need to be allowed some fluidity, and quibbling over sub-divisions at this time is unhelpful.

Bill

I would prefer no term at all as the stigma attached to both would be detrimental to my goals. However, in my own mind and anonymous discussions, I only use the term psychopath.

The term sociopath, at least to me, insinuates some degree of detachment from reality. I don't mean in the schizophrenic or psychotic sense of detachment.

Sociopaths are detached from the reality of their behavior and consequence and are often unable to take calculated risk.

A psychopath, at least one with some degree of intelligence, is well aware of a behavior and its risk. They can calculate the risk vs reward and make a more logical strategic plan for their long-term success. I see sociopaths as beneath the psychopath. A more simple analogy, I am the Lion a sociopath is a mere hyena.

The term psychopath and sociopath are most commonly understood to be the Ted Bundy's and

BTKs [6] of the world. The common person conjures ideas of serial killers and sadist after hearing those words. There are those even in the psychiatric profession that are proponents of indefinite institutionalization of psychopaths.

I have achieved what I have by being your neighbor, your friend, your leader and your role model. A label such as psychopath would make achieving those relationships significantly more challenging.

Dianne
Can you describe how you found out you were a psychopath or sociopath? Was it through on line searching or a professional analysis and can you explain in more detail about this searching?

How did you go about finding someone to do the evaluation, was it difficult and did you have to go to a few people to find the right one to diagnose you?

Fred
In terms of your question re: how I and why I found the information; I think in the midst of my madness, I wanted to find something to make sense of things. In a state of emotional shut-down I think I may have wanted it to be the case.

Partly because it was "any answer is better than none," but also I think because if I could stop

---

[6] "BTK" stands for "Bind, Torture, Kill," the infamous signature of serial killer Dennis Rader, who murdered ten people in and around Wichita, Kansas, between 1974 and 1991.

feeling, then the looming crash and subsequent mess would hurt less. In that state, I started applying it as a re-explanation of past behavior.

This is a danger with mental health as it is easy to impose a narrative on things if you're looking for it, whether it is really there or not. Therefore, a diagnosis based on purely retrospective criteria is liable to be shaky at best, I suspect. A diagnosis would need not only explanatory but also predictive grounding. Does that make sense?

I found information on the Internet in all the usual places: Wikipedia, forums, medical or mental health sites, etc. Much of it is useless, to be perfectly honest. However, reading accounts gave an interesting and new perspective from which to view the drier, more technical stuff.

Steve

A professional analysis has been done under another name of course, but I did start my search on-line to see if I fitted the profile. There are tests on-line too, but they are only 10% of the real test so not worth going by alone.

Finding out came with problems of its own because there is no way to fix this condition. However, it did help me to know why things kept going the way they did and better ways to hide it.

Dianne
Can you please clarify by what you mean by 10% of the real test? How did you go about finding someone to do the

evaluation, was it difficult and did you have to go to a few to find the right one?

I am asking because I am interested in the process of finding someone capable of doing the evaluation.

Steve
In the tests on the Internet there are 40 questions or less, and the real test is about 400 questions long. I cannot give you an exact number because it was about two years ago, and I just don't remember.

I had the test organized through a therapist whom I found that dealt with anger problems, but you can buy the test over the net, but it is not cheap. Look up "PCL-R."[7]

Bill
I have received a formal diagnosis and found the study through an acquaintance at a university in Vancouver that was looking for subjects. It piqued my interest so I arranged for my brother and me to fly to Vancouver.

Outside of a research team in Vancouver, I have never been called a psychopath. The interaction I had with the research group was primarily

---

[7] The Hare Psychopathy Checklist-Revised (PCL-R) is a psychological assessment tool developed by Dr. Robert Hare, used to assess the presence of psychopathy in individuals. It is a 20-item inventory of perceived personality traits and recorded behaviors, completed through a semi-structured interview along with a review of 'collateral information' such as official records.

interviews spread out over three days with three different interviewers.

It was not simply read off of the PCL-R checklist, but it was obvious that the questions were designed to gauge the 20 criteria.

Each interviewer asked several questions and while each interviewer had different questions, they were of the same categories. I am assuming they did this to see if there was a fluctuation in the PCL-R score between the interviewers. The also asked several questions about my brother and I would assume he was asked questions about me.

The questions I was asked about him, which again I assume he was asked the same ones, were primarily how he has reacted to certain situations in the past as well as how I would predict he would react to various scenarios.

Weeks before interviewing me, they asked permission to contact family members for an interview, and I allowed them to contact my mother only. She received a short questionnaire via mail.

The questions ranged from asking about my reactions to deaths in the family, unexplained death of pets, and childhood behavioral problems.

I was very tempted, throughout this process, to manipulate the results. Personality tests and the psych exams for employment are a hobby of mine to manipulate.

However, I can say, I withstood the temptation and answered my questions as honestly as possible. Mainly because my curiosity was stronger than my desire to manipulate the results.

As for the Canada interviews, the interviews took place in my hotel room. They sent one interviewer a day for three days. They were all doctoral students who had received some training on the PCL-R.

It was interesting listening to them describe their credentials. Graduate school here, bachelors from there, researched this and studied that...etc. I assume they were attempting to garner some trust in their abilities.

The questions differed from each interview, but they were obviously scripted to some degree. I can't remember all the questions, but most were along the lines of "What would you describe as your strengths...weaknesses."

They would ask about a personal situation, such as my father leaving or a family member's death, and ask me to describe the feeling I had about them.

What was most interesting is that some of the interviewers remained stoic and expressed zero reactions to anything I said. The others had strong reactions, almost theatrical. In retrospect, I wonder if they were trying to see if I would mirror these reactions.

The interviewer's personalities were drastically different. Some would be emotionally unavailable, acting as if they really didn't want to be there.

Others were empathetic to my "struggles" in life and seemed to genuinely care. I believe this too was scripted.

If you look at the PCL-R list of personality traits, the questions followed the list verbatim. It was easy to tell what each question was attempting to gauge. After asking questions about me, they asked almost the exact same questions to me about my brother.

Fred

I would like to say that I am not diagnosed by professionals. However, much of my behavior fits very well and the two most commonly used tests available to me (i.e. without involving professionals) put me in that sort of area.

I have also had many comments over the years as to certain events in which I've been accused of psychopathic/sociopathic behavior.

I seem to have some bipolar[8] features, and the degree of my behavior is significantly – although not solely – linked to this. Similarly, certain substances have a similar impact.

For example, caffeine and pot not only have the stereotypical motivated/ demotivated effects, but also change the severity of damage I'm likely to cause at any given time. This could be seen as "well, you are just plain doing more," but I think it is more than the more alert I am, the more easily I

---

[8] Bipolar disorder, formerly called manic depression, is a mental illness that brings severe high and low moods and changes in sleep, energy, thinking, and behavior.

get bored and feel the need for something interesting to happen.

With the bipolar, it is also not an official diagnosis. I'd be willing to stake significant money on both that and being a sociopath, though.

A couple of years ago, my mother confessed feeling somewhat guilty for never having got it checked when I was growing up, for fear of getting me labeled.

It is one of those few ironically wonderful moments when I really did mean it when I said she couldn't understand how grateful I was for that decision. I exhibit extremes. This may be incidental, rather than systemic.

However, I believe I do understand some aspects of emotion quite well. It is hard to tell though, as there is much I have learned to understand on a conceptual, not experiential, level.

I could convince you that I know what it is like to truly suffer. I could convince you I know what it is like to truly love. What would you to like me to understand best? I have learned the words and the faces for it all

Anyway, that's something of a tangent. Did it seem narcissistic? I find it hard to judge, but was going for wryly observational. Back on topic.

Dianne
I think your diagnosis of bipolar does provide an interesting element. It will make it much easier to get people to accept

odd behavior, and any wobbles will be easily overlooked.

There are a couple of reasons for that; as I mentioned before, it is a popular diagnosis these days so that means it gets tossed around a lot. It also is not that well understood unless a person was to go the extra mile and study the issue.

I base my opinion much more on knowledge; my instincts clearly play a role in most things, but that is not the only method that I use to determine if a person is indeed a psychopath.

I have had a lot of contact with them over the years, and there are certain characteristics that make it possible for me to determine if they are or are not. As they say, this isn't my first rodeo. There have to be common threads to identify behavior.

Fred
I have never sought help for bipolar because medication is something I have tended to avoid, unless prefixed with "self" (self-medicated). I've no problem screwing around with my mind to re-arrange things better to my tastes.

It's my mind, after all. I have to live in it. What medication strikes me as is allowing other people to re-arrange my mind to better suit their tastes. So long as I am not obviously harming anyone unduly, why should I not be whomever I please?

I would then be pandering to the neurotic sensibilities of society just so it didn't have to face the parts of itself; it finds uncomfortable.

Dianne
At what stage of your life and approximate age did you start to think there was something different about you and the world around you?

Can you explain how you went about figuring out you might be a psychopath?

Were there things that you read that brought you to that conclusion and led you to get a diagnosis?

I am assuming you had a good idea what the diagnosis was going to be so my question is kind of broad in terms of what were some of the triggers that got you thinking in that direction?

Steve
I was 11 when I knew I was not like other people because I saw someone die in front of me, and then everyone was so upset about it, and I didn't see why.

My mother thought that I was traumatized and holding it in but there was no feeling on my part at all about it. Unfortunately, everyone else involved was very upset so I started to stand out. I did go to their funeral because I didn't dislike them so then people calmed down, but that was the first time.

A year later, a girl drowned, and it was not me, by the way, but I had to try to pretend that I was shocked about it. It was hard to do because I knew that someone would probably drown there as it had no fences and a steep bank.

So she died, end of the story, but people seem to try to make it their fault and beat themselves up about it so her father went mad from it and her mother now drinks a lot.

It's funny people talk about honoring their memory....... But they never think if they are looking down that maybe you're upsetting them by doing things that hurt yourself if they cared and all?

I only thought I might be this way because of girlfriends telling me; everyone else just thought I was reserved about what I felt.

Dianne
From your description of the area where this girl drowned, it was a somewhat dangerous location, so I can see why the parents might blame themselves; however, it sounds like an accident. Was this a common play area?

Steve
It was not a common play spot, but it was easy to get to, and she couldn't swim.

Dianne
Do you believe in heaven?

Steve
I don't really believe in heaven or a god, but I tend to pretend to in order to go unnoticed or to make people trust me. The whole thing doesn't make sense to me because if someone saw everything, then why do people get away with doing all kinds of crap to each other?

I mean " it's all for a reason " is not cutting it for me. Plus the contradictions are too numerous in religion.

Dianne
Can you describe in more detail those defining moments when in reflection, you can see that you were not behaving the same as others?

Bill
The defining moment, that is a tough one. As I mentioned before, in hindsight I can think of several examples from my youth that could have clued someone in on my condition. I saw this again in Iraq, but to a much larger degree.

The things that had detrimental impacts to my fellow Marines didn't faze me.

I had no moral conflicts or disgust in the lack of humanity of war. At this point, there was no doubt, I was different.

This is when my focus shifted from being socially awkward to growing my skills and emotional mirroring. It took no time at all really; I was soon everyone's friend. This realization and the building of these skills opened whole new doors. I got out of the military and pursued professional goals. Which leads me to where I am today.

The light bulb for me was when I was in the service, stationed in Iraq. In one particular instance, a truck approached the perimeter of our observation point. As we began broadcasting warnings to slow and wait at the check point, we noticed the truck continuing and picking up speed.

Several people in the vehicle began firing in our direction. It didn't take much for us to disable the vehicle, a single 50 caliber shot to the engine block.

As the vehicle died, the occupants evacuated and continued in on foot. As they got in close enough range to be dangerous, we realized they were not all men. Some of them were young. I would guess in their teens. Nevertheless, they were there to kill as many as they could. Not the smartest tactic, to attack a post of Marines with a small band of men and teens armed with antiquated rifles.

Long story short, none of them were successful and none made it out alive. My job, as a medic, was to now go check for survivors and treat whoever I could. As I'm checking for vital signs, I notice members in my team teary eyed, saying prayers, or shouting in anger that anyone would send teenagers.

Me, I had headphones in one ear (listening to the song from "RENT," "One Song Glory") and wondering if we were getting a food convoy that day.

And if the question is lingering in your mind let me answer it now; I did fire my weapon in self-defense. I am unsure if my shots did not strike anyone, nor do I care.

There were no feelings of pleasure from their deaths or any sense of excitement or satisfaction. I've seen death and murder close up while there.

Having this experience is why I cannot understand how it would appeal to anyone. I suppose, on a neurological level, that it is a form of control.

Dianne
From what I understand the conscience forms by the ages of 3 – 5, but I think it is really out of the chute, that it is a matter of being born that way and is not a choice.

Someone many years ago posted something that stuck with me, along the lines that perhaps the parents don't reject or are repelled by the child, but the child is the one doing the rejecting.

I think it is the try harder concept; the more educated the parents are, the more they will correct and work with the child. In less advantaged households, the child will be left to their own devices and likely turn toward the criminal aspect.

Fred
Something that has been said of me many times over the years, by teachers and so forth when I was growing up, is that I don't have a malicious or

intentionally cruel bone in my body. I honestly believe this to be the case.

I've got SO much I can contribute and improve. But no, I'm too dangerous, presumably because of how I was born but to be honest I think it is nature AND nurture that plays a part.

Genetic predispositions that are then modified over time based on environment. Maybe I have the gene, but had such a loving upbringing that it was mitigated. Maybe I don't, but my upbringing was so disturbed that the traits were exaggerated.

I was havoc in my teens. The embodiment of chaos. Not evil. Chaos. Learning the rules to the games that didn't make any sense and nobody seemed to be playing well anyway. I mean... you run a support site for the victims of psychopaths.

How do you think I was to be around back then, as student, friend, son or role model? The only time I was allowed in the Home Economics classroom after the first year of secondary school was when I'd been thrown out of German again and there were exams, so I couldn't just be left in a corridor.

Bill
I was certainly well liked as a child; I just had little interest in doing what the popular kids did after school. Sports did not excite me, and I only went to the parties when I needed someone new to sleep with. I was very well-liked by the teachers. I was often able to get extensions on assignments, extra credit, or convince them to grade on a curve.

I was in advance placement for math and science and President of the Future Business and Career Leaders of America. I was also President of a Christian club; I can't remember the name of that one.

I had a following of friends. They waited by my locker for me in the mornings and often came over to my place after school.

I actually hated most of them. Unfortunately, I needed them. I knew early on; I couldn't get very far by not being "friendly."

I say I wasn't popular because I didn't really do much outside of school, other than what I felt was required to maintain my group of friends.

In hindsight, I can notice the difference as a young teenager. At the time, I didn't realize the difference. I think the biggest "wake-up call" was during my time in Iraq.

It's interesting; I was not very popular as a child. I now understand this to be caused by my unusual emotional reactions to things. My emotional expressions never really fit into the norm.

Dianne
Are you aware of any other psychopaths or sociopaths in your family history?

Steve
My father and my father's father had the same outlook as me. My brother is not nor is my mother.

Bill
If it is genetic, I would assume I would have got it from my father.

Dianne
Tell me about your relationship with your family. Was your father in the home while you were growing up?

Do you think, deep down; your mom knows the truth? Some parents have thought, even knowing their child was a "budding" psychopath, that further socializing them would help them fit into society better.

And I suspect to also keep them off of death row. I admire parents who think like that, I marvel at their courage. I am not sure what I would have done.

Steve
My father was there the whole time I was growing up. We didn't talk much, but that could have just been me because I tend not to talk much, and I like my space. I was raised in the same house as him, but he doesn't make smart business decisions but in spite of that I would say he is successful in what he does he has a good income.

My mother stayed in contact with my brother but not me. I think I am close to her, but that's because we live in the same place now. I'm not sure what that means to me. Is it supposed to mean something more?

My mother doesn't know I am a sociopath, but she thinks my father is.

Fred
If we do indeed imprint and learn behaviors to mimic and compensate, as well as seek positions of advantage, my upbringing may be the answer. My mum's side of the family was very loving and socially minded.

They were also very generous. I learned the behaviors, saw value in integrating them but never connected them up properly. What do you think about this idea?

Do you see what I mean about the nature/nurture point? The "you have it or you don't" angle seems so overly reductive, especially if there are neurological, developmental and genetic factors that can all stack in a variety of ways.

For example, I'd stake every penny I have on my dad having most of not all the genetic markers and a lot of the developmental ones, but not all the neurological ones. Frankly, I'm now convinced he's BPD [Borderline Personality Disorder], but the 'warrior gene' stuff is almost pouring off of him, as it were. That suggests I may well have it, but my upbringing was the total opposite.

That's my position on it, and I don't think I'll bother with a proper diagnosis as I'm no danger and don't want to be marked for life with some half-baked label that feeds from a fire of social ignorance.

Regarding the parents' thing, I think it is guilt. They will never, ever be able to reconcile the following things at the same time:

1) He's my son, and I love him.
2) He's my son, and he is incapable of returning that love in kind.
3) I might have played a part in making him that way.

And the obvious contender for (4) is "and is it in me, too?" Of course, they're reluctant to talk. If they said it aloud, they'd have to listen to it. Verbalizing – or writing down – things make them more real to people. Trans-hemispheric relay short-cut, it cuts out the crappy buffer nature gave us and lets us understand things differently than if we'd just thought them.

It's like increasing bandwidth so you can see everything in HD. If you want to, that is. I can see why they may not.

I do not think my family members know. It is actually the idea of them finding out that terrifies me - yes; I do mean that.

I love my family very much. My brother is a wonderful human being - unquestionably better than me, which I would say even when I'm feeling my most arrogant - and the idea of any of them suffering causes me great distress.

Bill
Do I suspect my parents knew? No. I came from a loving home and was never abused in any way.

While in my teens, I did use my parents a bit for money or whatever I wanted.

But it wasn't a particularly strict household, so lying wasn't really required. My grandfather spoiled me a lot growing up, so stealing wasn't really necessary either.

My brother and I have different fathers. My father left when I was a young child. So no, I'm not close to him. I am most honest with my mother. I don't really lie to her. We live on opposite sides of the country.

I joined the military at 17 and never moved back home again. I fly my mother out to my home every year or so. We have a small business together, which she runs in my absence.

My mother divorced my father after he cheated. My mother is a strong woman, so it doesn't surprise me that she would have the strength to divorce him. My father stayed in contact with me off and on until I was about 10 I guess.

He did marry another woman who already had two children. He never paid a dime of child support and had several failed businesses. He put the businesses in his new wife's father's name in order to avoid child support and wage garnishment. About a year into this new marriage, he stopped talking to me completely.

Last I heard; he is divorced again and lives with his mother. If I did inherit the psychopath gene from him, I certainly got a more successful version.

This brings up a good a point about being different as a child.

My mother got a therapist for me after my father stopped contacting me. She says it was because she expected there to be some emotional trauma from the experience. I don't remember a lot about the sessions, but I do remember thinking they were not necessary.

I didn't feel any different after he left. I did, however, enjoy the attention. I had no desire to reconnect and even today he doesn't cross my mind.

I do have my own "code," if you will. There are certain things I won't do, unless under extreme circumstances. One of these is in regards to my mother and brother.

I am not always fair with them; this is true, but I never do anything that will hurt them either. This to me is close. As they are the only two this rule applies to.

Dianne
Do you encounter others in your life who you think are more like you? People often question what a psychopath will do in the presence of another; does it happen?

Would a male psychopath be attracted to the female version of you or the same sex as you?

Fred

A female psychopath that had confidence and superficial simplicity would be a very attractive prospect. I don't like being toyed with though, so in reality it'd either end up in a situation of eternal sporadic sparring - for fun, out of boredom, just because. I dunno.

Why does anyone do anything? I know there are lots of reasons for not doing things and people think about these a lot. Less attention is paid to why they do the things that they do, in fact, do - or open war.

There's definitely some degree of recognition, if only a "so you're a bit like me, are you?" sort of thing. Other times it is pretty obvious. In people, I don't see often, it is harder to tell, since it may be a flash of BPD [Borderline Personality Disorder] or something else.

I understand there is substantial overlap in the definition of behaviors, so this would make sense. I'd also long considered myself 'normal' (I don't mean average, obviously. Just not this), so 'a bit like me' was all I had to go on, for the most part.

 One of my friends' dads growing up most certainly was one, but not hugely high functioning. I got on quite well with the guy; he was very funny and very intelligent. Sadly, he was also very bad at hiding his constant frustration and contempt, which meant brief interaction, was fine, but we avoided each other for any lengthy engagements. I'm fairly sure he knew what I am, even if I didn't realize it myself at the time.

I had one ex that is definitely somewhere on the spectrum, but so far along the narcissistic axis that she makes mistakes because she's so full of herself. She's got no idea I am, but mostly because every time we hook up, I leave her with a mewling idiot letter or rant, studded with messages she overlooks.

She thinks all men have been 'ruined by their mother' anyway, which is why I do them; I know it will make her go away for a while, but retain her interest should I desire it again. I don't expect to hear anything from her for a while yet though.

I think she's still mad about the last time, when victory suddenly turned out to have been a mirage. My play-collapse is totally out of place and to be honest; she should realize that by now.

However, she also thinks she has the key to my heart, because that was what she wanted to have, so I made sure she believes she has it. She's a lot of fun, and I'm not afraid of her, but I'm not utterly stupid either. It'd be like playing all six seats in a game of Russian roulette.

Yeah, you might win five times in a row and then be able to bow out. But you're probably going to decorate the place with the ruins of your very favorite possession.

There is always going to be an element of narcissism. A need to show off. In many cases, there is pleasure in being feared as something 'other', beyond the Ken of mortals. There is also at least a fairly free & easy approach to the truth. This is not to say that it is all lies, but that it is worth considering if it is being played up in order to get a particular reaction.

Nobody wants to be boring to others, least of all a narcissist. The idea of someone so intelligent, so capable of manipulating human behavior and so remorseless as to not care is like some sort of 21st century vampire, with the perceived glamour and mystique that goes with it.

On this basis, I would caution against letting any of the people you are interviewing from trying to make you focus too heavily on one area or another.

Does it happen? Of course, it does. How integral/extreme/planned is it? That's likely to vary. Some will try to hide the extent of their actions; others will exaggerate them.

I don't know what the others are getting out of their exchanges, but it's a fair bet that in some form or other it will include self-aggrandizement.

Love me, fear me... it doesn't really matter which, so long as you pay me attention, and I can interpret it as adulation.

(The "I" above is similar to the general "you" I specified earlier, rather than my personal responses to these things. I'm trying very hard to be as honest as I possibly can be, and I think I'm doing a fairly good job of it.)

Bill
I have not really researched the interactions of psychopaths with other psychopaths or their

ability to identify one another. My instinct is to believe that it would be difficult for them to identify one another.

Since most of our understandings of feelings came from playing off cues of those who have them, I would imagine convincing another psychopath that I feel would be easy.

They have no real way of knowing if my "emotional" responses are normal as they are simply playing off my imitation of emotions.

The particular person in my office, who I suspect of being psychopathic, played right into my manipulation. They played into it, and it paid off for me for years until they stopped.

This relationship was mutually beneficial. It has come to the point now where our interests oppose one another. This is where I began to see behind the mask. It has certainly set the stage for an upcoming battle of epic proportions.

The trick, the fun, will be to win without damage to my credibility. It's a real challenge. While it is work, I enjoy this because this will not be as simple as anything I've done before. As far as being able to keep up, I have no doubt I will prevail.

As far as attractiveness, you are absolutely right. Those who are more attractive certainly have an advantage. I am in good shape, but I could never be a model.

Physical traits help with first impressions and if coupled with an appealing personality or mask, can have free reign in the office. These are all superficial attractions on the part of the "normal" people feeding into the attractive person.

My ability to be NEEDED is much more efficient and productive in the longer run.

Dianne
Others have said they wanted to learn because certain things and patterns kept happening, and they weren't quite sure exactly how to pinpoint them.

Have you had much time to read the comments from victims at my discussion forum and if so were there any areas that drew your attention more than others?

There are many discussions about how victims see the eyes, sex and a variety of things.

Would you like to start the conversation by answering some of the above and then seeing what attracts your attention the most for us to explore?

Bill
I suppose my interest in other psychopaths and their victims is my admiration for a clever manipulation. Additionally, the most disastrous of my failures have always included me encountering another psychopath in my climb up the ladder.

If I don't recognize them soon enough I waste valuable time attempting to establish that "bond" that is needed for a successful manipulation.

When I come across a psychopath in a position that I want, it sets the stage for a clash of the titans. This is a challenge I am currently facing.

These conflicts can eventually spill out into public view, creating attention that is not beneficial to either side. This creates the need for a different strategy altogether.

A psychopath, on the other hand, will display a character that isn't his (or less commonly, hers). Leading you to believe in weaknesses that aren't there. Identifying this person early would provide me with a distinct advantage.

However, I don't think I have ever looked at someone and thought "yup he is in the club." I look for weaknesses or areas to exploit when I meet people. I would assume that those I have difficulty spotting a weakness could be a psychopath.

Think of it this way; what I identify as a weakness is often an emotion. Whether it is depression, loyalty, pride, anger, it's all an emotional response. Your weakness is your emotion.

A psychopath does not have this weakness. If I cannot find a readily available weakness, I will often look to another target.

Perhaps these people I pass over are the psychopaths? This is an interesting concept, one I will have to play around with and see if it has a practical application in my office.

If there were a Psychopath Club, I wouldn't imagine it would have a lot of rules. I certainly think we would be profoundly productive working together toward a common goal.

The problem I would see in this is there is obviously no loyalty. I would absolutely turn on them to save myself or to increase my own profits.

The discussions at your forum regarding psychopaths and fear as well as the posts regarding sex with a psychopath are of particular interest to me. I found this comment at your forum quite interesting:

> "The psychopath who was in my life used to show high anxiety by flushing bright red about the face and neck, and his fingers, hands and feet would almost hammer whatever they were touching to near destruction.
>
> As for what would cause the anxiety, that could be something like putting on a great public face while wanting to behave in an abusive way - almost like it being so hard to contain himself that the real him is bursting out of his skin and feet.
>
> Incidentally - taking a look under the table at the manic movement of a psychopath's feet is quite an eye opener!
>
> How can they move their feet so fast yet keep their upper half so 'normal' looking!"

This was posted under the section (forum thread) of "Do Psychopaths Feel Fear." What your member is explaining here is not anxiety or fear. It is their attempt at impulse control.

The primitive emotion of anger is the downfall of psychopathy. It's the one thing we often have difficulty controlling. I experience this sensation at almost every single board meeting.

To resist the urge to come "unhinged" at stupidity or from an accusation (often a true one), is felt physically. Knowing the outburst would be counter-productive, I do all can to contain it. This control is becoming easier.

There are days, especially days where I'm tired or have already experienced setbacks, where this impulse control is particularly difficult. It is also interesting to hear the perception of some actions I could be seen doing. Such as this post.

Dianne
A tragic bank robbery here took the lives of several innocent people. They were shot point blank as the blameless customers entered the bank. It had and still has a huge impact on this small community. The robbers didn't even steal any money.

Fortunately, they were caught within a couple of hours while eating at a fast-food restaurant. In the trial, the ringleader claimed that he was a psychopath and should not be held responsible for this horrific crime.

Clearly, his rationale didn't work as they are all locked up for good. The one person who may not have been a psychopath was the getaway driver; he left the scene. Fortunately, in the eyes of the law, that still made him as guilty as the ones that did the killing.

The criminals who murdered all those innocent people are of no interest to me. I wouldn't waste my time traveling to prison to interview them.

All the public is focused on is psychopathy and murder; I have expanded my thinking over the years.

I find non-criminal psychopaths more interesting than those who murder, as they are a greater challenge to identify.

Bill
I tend to agree with your take on the violent psychopaths. In it is not the psychopathic condition that causes them to murder. It may be a conduit, allowing them to kill without remorse, but there are almost always identifiable factors, outside of psychopathy, that lead to the murders. For example, John Gacy.[9] Was he a psychopath, I'm sure he was.

Was it psychopathy that caused him to murder boys and place them beneath his floorboards? No. Was it psychopathy that allows him to do it without guilt? Yes. So while psychopathy is a key

---

[9] John Wayne Gacy, Jr., also known as The Killer Clown, was a convicted American serial killer and rapist who sexually assaulted and murdered at least 33 teenage boys and young men between 1972 and 1978 in Chicago, Illinois.

component, it is an accomplice and not the key perpetrator.

CHAPTER THREE
Self Image: Good versus Evil

"Words, like nature, half reveal and half conceal the soul within."
—Alfred Lord Tennyson

Dianne
Tell me how you would describe yourself. Do you think you are a good person?

Steve
I have some redeeming features; for starters I try to not be violent in my dealings and not to have my partners living in fear. Just because I'm controlling and manipulating does not mean that I'm cruel or sadistic.

Fred
I do not know if I am a good person or a bad person. Am I a good person who is bad at it? Am I a bad person who tries to be good?

And maybe, just maybe, I'm sometimes a genuinely decent guy by normal standards. I'd argue that is all anyone is that I'm just more self-aware. Not in the social sense, perhaps, but in what answers I find when I look at myself. Who do you see? "Oh I dunno.

I guess someone who just wants to love life and find someone to share the journey with.", "A gentle, kind heart who is a little scared of being hurt," "and a lonely wanderer just looking for answers like everybody else." No. I don't know. Maybe nothing.

I do not believe myself to be a bad person. Mostly, I think I act with fairly benign intent, and most of the damage is caused when people get in too close and expect to find something different from what is the case.

It's like I'm covered in hooks and fluffy people stick to me, only to be shredded by the process of being torn free again.

But if you ask me why I am doing something; the honest answer is usually going to be 'because I feel like it', 'because it interests me' or 'because that is the best answer' or similar.

I am, whatever you may think, not thoroughly callous, cruel or uncivilized. I even enjoy being pleasant, kind, 'normal' in a way. Doubly so when I'm also able to 'be myself' at the same time.

If you find my previous reasons insufficient, you could very well add, "Because it has value to me" or "Openness is a novelty" to the list. It doesn't change anything, but it is true.

It seems that just as I was starting to feel confident I'm a decent person; I have to confront the fact that in many ways I am not. Even when I'm trying really, really hard to be a good one.

As I mentioned before, this is something of a discovery process for me. I believe that I'm (very? I think so) high functioning in that my upbringing piled on lots of 'positive' social stuff and some of it stuck.

The first imprints. My master copies. What I've most often fallen back on. That means that outside closer personal relationships, it is unlikely anyone would ever have reason to suspect anything or fear that I'll cause them any hurt. I seem like a well-adjusted, somewhat 'sketchy', easy-going, confident, generous person.

Supportive, too. Very supportive. Everyone comes to me when they have really serious problems. I think because my advice is good, and I know them well enough to couch it in terms that make sense for them as an individual.

How good is that wording? I mean, really... doesn't it sound so much better, than "I reflect the image of them that can deal with the problem effectively and without too much guilt"? They mean the same, though. In either direction.

Bill
Have you heard the term Puppet Master, in relation to psychopaths? If you were to further classify psychopaths, this is the category which best describes my tendencies.

Dianne
Many people say psychopaths are evil. What are your thoughts about that?

Fred
I hope I have not so far conformed to the "vile & evil" (I do so love words) expectations. It is interesting to think differently like this, so for my

part I am enjoying our conversation. It's okay; that's not a prompt to reciprocate. I mean, it is. But it isn't. That is not its function on this occasion.

I'm not a monster. Nobody dies; nobody goes bankrupt. I look bored at weddings and don't say 'no' when someone I care about asks me to make them happy. But 'evil', 'chilling', 'heartless'.

Dianne
Perhaps the vile and evil come from our difference. You may view vile and evil in a context that I don't understand. To help me answer your question as why people think in terms of fear of what a psychopath may do instead of what they are doing if I have the question correctly. If you can give me what do you think vile and evil is?

Bill
Evil, this is a fascinating term. One that I believe has no real application in the modern age. A term used to describe what people refuse to believe is in human nature. I'm certain you will disagree so I ask, what qualifies to be called evil?

How can I, a man who has never killed anyone, be evil if evil is described as the bank robbery you write about? I would assume, for you, evil is found more in the intent of an action as opposed to the action itself. To this, I respond, my intent is never to financially/professionally harm anyone.

> When I am targeting a currently occupied position my goal is not to harm the incumbent. I simply want them out of the way. Whether they are harmed in the process or find a better job elsewhere is of no concern. Granted, the former is more often the case. So what is the intent here?

Why would that be called evil? Is it not ambition, a trait I share with non-psychopaths?

Yes, you can't speak of psychopathy without speaking of murder. After all, this is what gets the headlines.

Murder is such a waste of a gift for a psychopath. I have yet to understand its appeal. The risk far outweighs any potential reward. I find it sloppy and the lowest form of failure.

In your story of the bank, I find it perplexing that the robber even considered it a worthwhile venture. The average haul from a bank robbery is minimal, and the risk is absurdly high.

Even if the heists were successful, the money could never be fully enjoyed in the way any psychopath would want to enjoy it. This is why I have no interest in violent crime. It is rarely successful, and I can obtain the same results without the violence or attention from law enforcement.

Fred

I'm not sure what you mean regarding vile/evil. They are anagrams of great elegance. 'Vile' is disgusting. Am I correct? Revolting. Evil is just that applied to human behavior. Evil is vile behavior. Ugliness. No? Yes? I mean, it definitely fits. The explanation works. Does it match your explanation, though?

That is my understanding of it. Good behavior = beautiful behavior. Bad behavior = ugly behavior. I'd be more certain, but it really doesn't match up with how everyone treats each other in practice.

Dianne
I am not sitting here judging, calling you vile or evil. In no way am I singling you out. You know what the purpose behind my writing about is: to discuss all sides of it. Here again, you could help me by explaining if you feel you have a conscience.

Fred
I'm not upset. I think I understand. Still, the point is an important one because it is precisely what I'm saying: the only difference is I know and accept it for what it is.

You cannot please all the people, all the time. Sometimes, you can't please anyone. It is just an unfortunate situation, and all involved need to take a long hard look at themselves. I would too, but I can't. You understand how it is; no soul.

That's not meant unkindly. But imagine it. Imagine being me. We are told to think for ourselves and then crucified when we do. I am aware that you do not mean what you say in a hostile manner. But that's the rub, isn't it?

What is the reality? All Xs are Y. Fred is an X; therefore, Fred is Y. Sociopaths, psychopaths, whatever term has been used; the debate is framed on the understanding; they are evil.

We are evil. I am evil. We talk of conscience, but are you not saying, "it's only business," too? "I mean in general," "as a whole," "typically." I.e.? Not. Personal. For the Greater Good.

As I've said before, I am not a bad guy. I'm less judgmental than most and because of my 'disability' (mental illness, a personality disorder); I just fall a tiny bit too far from the line of best fit that some shallow, arrogant jerk has drawn through social behaviors and labeled 'normal'.

That is all. Yet many people would treat me as a pariah, some sort of satanic missionary.

I probably do more for other people than any 20 average people combined, but because I can lash out and do some rather psychologically nifty stuff, I get labeled the anti-Christ and people - such as on your forum - are howling for my blood. I am not howling for theirs. I want them to be happy and find themselves.

I'd even throw myself into a relationship with them to try to help them become better, happier people. To avoid making the mistakes. I can solve their problems.

I feel good, today. I have found two good songs, so I am learning them. They have a good feel to them, manic. Totally unstoppable. One of them is by a band called The Pretty Reckless; Heaven Knows. The chorus is "Oh lord; heaven knows / we belong way down below."

Defiantly. Unrepentantly. Yes, that is where we will go, if we go anywhere at all. It is where everyone wants us to go. Nothing personal, of course. They just do. Why fight it? It isn't real anyway and even if it is, I am what I am. This is whatever someone makes me, for their own needs. They send me to hell. Pity. Hate. Satisfied by the idea. But I don't care.

They imagine themselves a victory because they are just as uncomfortable with the idea of defeat as I am.

The difference is that I only settle for a real one. Otherwise, I face the defeat and let it burn me until I learn from it. Improve.

The point is, I think the "you have it, or you don't" line isn't entirely accurate. People said the same about homosexuality and depression.

Nothing is ever that simple. Trust me; nothing is ever just black and white. People think it is because they think that 'true' means one thing and one thing only. It doesn't.

There's a whole spectrum of us. Some cruel and ruthless and feeding their partners medication to screw with them. Others well intended but confused and inadvertently destructive.

Is that me painting myself in a good light? No. I am committed to honesty here, and I mean to stick to it. That's my honest appraisal, and I would bet everything I own that I'm right on that. Without a second thought.

Dianne

I agree the issue is sticking to only seeing things in black and white and not allowing gray to be seen. I think like most things, there are many, many layers.

Perhaps it is the lack of gray along with the judgments that people put on things.

I think in the case of psychopaths it makes it easier for some to only see the black-and-white aspects; he/she can't possibly feel the same emotions as I do. Really? I don't know; I have absolutely no way of knowing;

I can barely keep track of my own emotions and have no capacity to be inside the mind of others, and if I did that would make me a super person. No one has that capability that I am aware of.

I can only say that we all have emotions, and everything is open to debate because we are separate and unable to crawl into the minds of others.

I can say from my interviews that we probably share a lot of things that might surprise some people who want to hang every psychopath at the stake.

Fred

Black and white are just directions, like left and right. We are not simply our genetics. We are an expression of how our genes interact with a dynamic, complex and increasingly abstract world.

Just because we have a gene that makes our eyes blue and another one that makes us angry or fearful doesn't mean that those genes are all equally dominant and inviolate.

Our minds can be understood as an error-checking mechanism to keep our genetics in check, because they can't evolve as quickly as the world does, and they lack purposive content beyond "survive and make more copies."

So we've developed something that can check the appropriateness of genetically predisposed responses against the current environment.

When you live in a cave and hunt the same plains as a sabre tooth tiger, the impulse to respond to suddenly have something charge at you by trying to kill it as quickly as possible is entirely appropriate.

When you live in a house and the most dangerous thing, you're likely to meet in any given year is a house cat, it is less so. But our genes don't know that, and that's why we're here to keep an eye on them.

I remember seeing a documentary some time ago (I believe you may have referenced it previously in our earlier emails, but I've really been through a mangle recently so please forgive me if I'm wrong) about a guy, who was doing research into psychopaths. Just out of interest, he did the genetic tests on himself and found he had the so-called "warrior gene" and lots of traits of psychopathy.

However, due to having a very loving, stable and supportive life, he was anything but; he was incredibly high functioning. Hence my seemingly unjustified insistence that I think it's more complicated than just "is or isn't." Or rather, if we're interested in the behavioral aspects, then we may need to separate them from the physiological ones.

Does it really matter what enables sociopathic or narcissistic behavior? I mean of course it does; it is of great interest and could provide huge benefits to all of us if we could work it out. But also, the causes themselves aren't a problem; it is the form of the expression of them.

Psychopathic behavior is the problem, not psychopathic genes or environments.

If someone with all the genetic markers for a real Patrick Bateman[10] type character can be a loving, happy family man with a successful career that is helping others greatly, it seems to me that clearly it is the behaviors that are the problem.

Rocks aren't problems, but the behavior of throwing rocks at others is.

There is also the question of what 'problem' is defined as and the fact we bring much to this

---

[10] Patrick Bateman is a character portrayed by Christian Bale in *American Psycho,* a 2000 movie. Patrick Bateman is a wealthy New York investment banker who hides his alternate psychopathic ego from his co-workers and friends as he escalates deeper into his illogical, gratuitous fantasies.

definition and then see it as part of what was there before we arrived.

You are right to point this out, as it is similar to the old adage of "one man's terrorist is another man's freedom fighter."

Dianne
Do you "put on a mask" to make yourself seem like other people? If so, is it a specific persona, or a composite person?

Fred
What you call a mask is not there to hide something; it is there to cover for an absence of something. Or, if there is something there at all, it is something primal; unbreakable will to self-interest and a hatred for anything that opposes it.

Situations that cause fear in an average person will instead inspire animal hatred and an overwhelming need to destroy the threat. This is the static that experiences either sooth (desirable) or antagonize intolerably.

What is behind the mask is either nothingness, surrounded by impulse-static. I discovered this by accident a good few years ago, although obviously, I didn't know what to call it or any context to give it other than "who I really am."

I've always been aware that I've sociopathic traits and this issue has, above all others, fascinated me, for as long as I can remember.

I do not know whether that void is where a 'normal' person should have grown. For a long-time – and to some extent, still now – I believed that everyone is this. I think this is important, as looking back over some of my behavior, at the time I sincerely believed I was only acting rationally, reasonably and in the way, other people would.

To me, I would have said others all wear masks, putting on performances of rituals that they label 'loving', 'caring', 'sharing', 'showing an interest', etc. They were being hypocrites in being hurt by my actions when they were doing the same themselves.

Use of emotional appeal against me is a form of blackmail and therefore, a hostile attempt to control. In retrospect this - with one exception - was probably projection on my part.

If I am to believe what people say about their own inner feelings, I could only really say that I am 'empty'. There is a very unpleasant feeling associated with any direct awareness of this emptiness/ nothingness and I believe that may be a motivator - at least in my personal case - towards constant stimulation.

I doubt it would be possible for me to communicate quite how intolerable boredom is. The closest I could get; I think, is that it feels like having my mind turned inside out in the presence of a dazzling, unbearably bright light.

Existential disorientation. Hell. In my personal flight-fight scale, boredom triggers both responses at maximum alert. It must be avoided.

And I believe that this 'nothingness' is why we can't be reasoned with, at least in normal terms. A normal person cannot predict and understand such people because there is nothing to understand, as they would see it.

All is immediacy, survival and advantage. Pirandello's Rules of the Game.[11] I believe these can be effectively leveraged without any gross 'moral misconduct' and I am rather proud of the degree to which I manage to do this, considering what I've come to realize is 'my nature'.

Not all of us are the same, but in terms of personal relationships, we are all to be avoided. We are not playing the same game.

Even when we are trying to keep some degree of calm around us, we will destroy things; incidentally, subconsciously, just out of habit.

My interest in all this is further self-understanding and development of ways to live with the minimum of disruption to my life. Over the years, I have learned this is best achieved by minimizing the disruption to the lives of those around me.

I left my best stuff in my other suit. The one that I wear for people to like me. Because that is what I

---

[11] The Rules of the Game is a play written in 1918 by Luigi Pirandello. The principal characters are Leone, his estranged wife Silia, and a man called Guido who is having an affair with Silia. Rather than allow himself to feel betrayed and angry, Leone chooses to empty himself of all emotion, becoming in his own words like an empty eggshell. He manipulates Guido into taking his place in a duel, in which Guido dies.

have to do; dress up to be liked. I've never tried just defaulting to 'skeleton crew' around anyone in person but I would bet you a small – or large – fortune that without me so much as saying anything they would find me unpleasant to be around. Don't fall for it.

Although, on one level, I know that it should be a sad thing. I can make a feeling that goes with it. Like a facial expression at myself (??). Just, if I think about it, it is quickly rationalized away as unimportant. I mean, it's only what I think everyone is doing all the time anyway, with added self-awareness.

I do not know why I should coo at babies. I have no idea why people think I want to see pictures of their childhood. I am usually very polite, courteous and charming in these situations simply because it has shown itself to be the best way of getting through them without being the target of some socially-manufactured outrage at my supposed shortcoming.

Why? Self-improvement, better understanding... many reasons. I don't mean that as some bid to sound virtuous, but simply to answer the floating "where this is going/what is the catch?" thoughts.

By composite people, I assume you mean a kind of 'average mask'; what they think is the best combination of features from all their masks. If so, then I quite agree.

I may be mercurial by nature, able to change masks more easily than normal people do, but I think there's an interesting counterpart to this.

I can choose to change them more easily, but can I choose not to change them, to make one so good that I can leave it in place? That'd be a grand trick, don't you think?

Something I could be really proud of, that would also solve many of my problems and the majority of the problems; I apparently cause other people.

I am not so much interested in a part-time mask. What I want is a formulation of me that can be lasting and permanent that is never removed nor accidentally dropped. Being bipolar may make that harder, but it may also make it easier.

My mercurial nature can be understood in bipolar terms rather than other terms; I can draw a line through the average and adopt that permanently as a sort of one size fits all solution. Any wobbles are down to bipolar, nothing more or less.

We all change our persona based on context, necessity and providence, so how would this be any different? Do you mean to say there is no 'real' me? Am I not a person at all, as opposed to merely a different person?

Bill
Try as I may to sympathize, I never think it is convincing. To counter this, I have created my personality to include a more "manly" response to empathy and appear to be the "rock" you can lean on.

This isn't ideal but I haven't mastered empathy as of yet, so it is the best I have for the time being. It is still a work in progress.

Dianne
Do other people seem to sense you're not being honest about your feelings?

Fred
I have been asked/told/accused many times how I can be so angry and then suddenly not be. I've noticed that it tends to be less disturbing to people when I'm venting my frustration than the switch to calmness and having 'forgotten about it' suddenly appears to.

It seems to destabilize them and damage self-esteem, which would match up with what you say regarding depression and value anchoring.

I am actually quite a fan of honesty. Preferably, in others, but my own can also help keep things simple and therefore, easier to control. There are in addition what I suppose I would label 'passive routines' of behavior; trust-winning, sincerity and so on. Sometimes they border on real, like a very, very weak radio signal.

Nothing that can't be ignored, but sometimes there. Like method acting, I suppose; imagine a situation where I would exhibit all the traits of 'sincerity' and be like that. It's a place. A window to look out of when you want a particular view.

I suppose 'remorse' is similar in that sometimes, after actions I can intellectually appreciate that I should not have done what I did. I don't really feel sorry for it, in the same way as I don't feel sorry when I make a bad move in chess.

I may be angry at having been distracted into making a mistake, but not 'sad'. This is a big part of the difficulty. Do I feel these things? I do not know.

Dianne
When you say you don't know if you feel these emotions, do you actually think about it? It seems as if you do not want to examine your own feelings.

Fred
People are mirrors. Some of us reflect more than others.

I have, many times over the years, including long before starting to realize what I may be, thought that the reason for much of my behavior is vicarious experience.

I cannot feel these things that you do, so I cannot understand them how you do. I have to learn by observation and experiment.

There is no manual to explain it, so we have to press buttons to find out how things work. I think there's also a process of then trying to press those buttons for ourselves and a sense of confusion when the same things don't happen.

Growing up we are told that as we're older, we will understand why people want to have kids, plan ahead, be part of a community. It continues not to happen, and eventually you realize that's because it isn't true.

You mention that there's the impression of lack of introspection. I think in some cases – such as mine, whatever that may be – that nothing could be further from the truth.

Firstly, since we are also supposed to be our very favorite topics, why wouldn't we be? Secondly, because of the contrast around us and our obviously different perspective on things, our nature in contrast to that of others is all the more strikingly of interest. Thirdly, we benefit more from introspection because we are less restrained in how we exercise its fruits.

Perhaps it is people being confused with 'self-aware', which it is possible I sometimes am not. Probably, due to some invisible convention of approval that I'm not a party to.

I was just with some people. Friends. I thought I'd watch me for a bit, instead of them. Nobody ever notices that while they're laughing at a joke, I look into the distance, grin and nod appreciatively.

It looks like laughter. Even better, it looks like laughter and having heard something witty enough to stand further consideration. Funny and clever. Good dog.

And had I not looked for it; I would not have even realized that was what I was doing.

Who is exploiting who, exactly? You tell me.

Do you see that, there? I caught it re-reading. In plain sight, right while I am telling you this is how it works, by letting others draw our faces and color our eyes, you tell me.

You want a lost little boy who wandered astray? How about haunted soul pining for the light? Just as confused by the world, scared and wanting answers as everyone else?

I do not mean that I am not interested in your thoughts on these things, for I am. In a sense, people may say what I am doing is 'baring my soul'.

However, in all honesty, my understanding of that could simply be to try to show you bits of your own. Watch my words. Even so, also do tell me if you think you notice it. I am curious as to how self-aware I could potentially learn to be.

And this is how we mirror. What do you want me to be? I can be it. How about you? I can be that too. Open up, let them be comfortable and the dreams quickly pour out. You care about the poor? Me too! Nobody understands you? I do.

Bill

I am not the "empty shell" of a human that is often portrayed in movies. Patrick Bateman, from *American Psycho*, gave the stereotypical impression of a psychopath. While it hinted at the truth, it missed the mark.

While it is certainly true, I lack the emotional experience of life, I am not unaware that emotions exist.

From an intellectual, level I am aware that if certain things are done, you would be hurt, mad, upset...etc. I understand the meanings of these emotions and can plan and/or react accordingly.

When I see an emotional reaction, I do not instinctually realize the reason for such a reaction, as you may. I must analyze the situation, understand the actual events, and arrive to a logical conclusion as to why the person reacts.

This is all done very quickly although I would venture to guess that it would not be as quickly as your emotional insight would provide you with the answer.

In American Psycho, Bateman says that he appears human but on the inside he is "simply not there." I do not agree with that expression. I am there; I have thoughts, plans, goals and wants. I think, therefore, I am. If you were able to see inside of me, you would see all these things.

Obviously, you would notice things missing. This just leaves me lacking certain aspects of humanity, not empty. Whether or not I have a soul is a topic of religious debate.

Dianne
The best explanation I can give is that what divides us is I have a conscience, and you don't; so for example, if I had to do something like by being ordered in time of war to kill, I would probably struggle for a lifetime with the inhumanity that goes along with war.

Since you have no conscience, you would very likely not miss a beat. I do believe it is in the human condition or part of it, but I refuse to believe that the entire society is evil.

It is the evil that lacks a conscience that interests me very much.

Fred
I do feel I have a conscience, but I do not know if you would feel I do. I am very, very concerned with morality.

I have an intellectual capacity to understand that some things are Done and some things are Not Done. I understand that convention dictates that when you act in ways that are Not Done then you feel ill. It gets called 'bad', but whatever. Negative reinforcement.

I can understand – better than you might imagine – how all the moral rules fit together. I just don't feel ill when I break them. Well, none of those that I have broken or expect to ever break, at least.

Extremes? Hard to say. Exceptional circumstances and I doubt an average person would be able to really say, either. It'd be something like "well, I'd hope I'd feel..." which is really "I would currently not do that and cannot imagine doing so, but shall just go right on ahead and assume the best of myself." No shit. Me too.

A good thief can sneak in and then escape the guards. A great thief can sneak in and out without alerting the guards. The best thief, though, is paying the guards. Because it is his house, and they are his valuables. He doesn't need to steal for anything other than the thrill anymore. That's why he's the best.

Maybe it is fair to say that I do have a conscience, but only in the same way as somebody with color blindness can still see things. Just because they don't have the right - or maybe any - colors to them doesn't make them invisible.

Now that I think of it, most predators operate in monochrome and differentiate things based on movement rather than coloration. I may have analogized my way to the truth of the matter, quite by accident. I hope not though, because that's quite a boring answer.

I do have moral awareness and reactions and do not feel the need to explain them in terms of consequences (indeed, I think consequentialism[12] and its equally philosophically popular stepchild, utilitarianism,[13] are profoundly flawed and dangerous foundations for ethical judgment).

The point is, without thinking about these things from an emotionally detached position it is far more difficult to realize these 'deeper truths'.

Emotions, when they're heavily involved in our mental processes, distort our reasoning to at least

---

[12] Consequentialism is the doctrine that the morality of an action is to be judged solely by its consequences

[13] Utilitarianism is the doctrine that actions are right if they are useful or for the benefit of a majority; essentially, when the end justifies the means.

some extent. They are immediate and seem very, very important, so demand that they be taken account of and obeyed.

That means we don't necessarily give the time and consideration to what is going on in the background, what underlies the whole thing. Or, in other words, they make it harder to shift perspective and find new ways of understanding things.

I've studied ethics quite extensively, having written a little on the subject. This also helps me 'pass for normal,' I think. In some ways, maybe I'm half a normal person. Like the shell of a house.

Are there parts of the house? Yes. Is it, in actuality, a house? I think not. It was never finished. The bits where all the living happens are missing, if I understand my own metaphor correctly.

Dianne
You say that you feel like half a normal person, like the shell of a house. Is it emotions that you are missing? Do you feel any emotions about anything?

Fred
In part, there seem to be elements to houses that are 'finished' that I lack but are apparently enjoyable. I like enjoyment. Who doesn't? That's what it means: 'this is something I like'.

It also makes people think themselves superior to me by their very nature, which I dislike. Do not enjoy.

I could take them on a visit to my home turf and let them see how they fare when they are the visitor. Have done. You know how it ends. But what does that really prove?

That I can beat people at a game they can't understand but that has been my life. So... what if I could beat them at the game, they play themselves? The one where I'm playing with a handicap.

If it is possible, then I am intelligent enough to learn. I am not so far from the fold, as these things go. I have said to you, I believe, that part of winning is showing to be dominant, victorious, and superior over that individual.

If I could do that to society as a whole, we would all be getting what we want. Without the ever-presented destruction and all the bullshit that comes with it.

And, more importantly in some ways, knowing myself that I've done something that others in similar positions find too difficult. Be king on both sides of the border. Oh! And understand more. So much more. Understanding is good. In many ways, it is power.

Riches are just power. Love is just what people call another kind of power. Both give the same results; extensions of your will into the world, enabling you to better solve problems and supply needs. I mean what do other people think the third thing is? Vanilla, chocolate and... strawberry? It's all just ice-cream.

It seems likely that a sense of victory is linked to the power issue. Neurologically, I can only assume that my reward centers — however, they may be arranged — are only triggered by 'did best' rather than 'did well'.

You may ask whether my sense of grandiosity skews those even further, requiring very extreme victories to satisfy. You'd be right to do so, because if I have a narcissistic view, then surely I crave unrealistic degrees of victory? Well, not unrealistic. Unrestrained.

So do I tone down my expectations, in case they are grandiose? Only if I want to live with no pleasure at all.

Also, I can lose. If I don't care about something, I'll not put any effort into it. Ah. Okay, that's not entirely true. I'll not be seen to put any effort into it. However, it doesn't really bother me. Why allow other people's interests to control me in such a way?

They care about winning whatever it is — at golf, say — and that is fine. I do not though and will not allow myself to feel slighted by others setting the victory conditions. Perhaps unusually,

I dislike cheating intensely. If I have engaged in a game, I shall show I am better at it on the same terms as others. So there is no doubt in their minds about it.

Other person cheating upsets this and makes me look like a poor loser when I catch them at it, which does not go down well. Obviously, in areas other people wouldn't consider 'games', things are a bit different.

They would say I am cheating. I would say they are merely playing badly.

I shall always feel the need to censor myself to some extent. I have seen what happens when I do not. In many ways, I am freer than most people; I suppose. Being able to 'be myself' is not one of those things. There quite possibly isn't a 'myself' to be, and even if there was I cannot imagine it would be welcome.

There is also what may be grief of my own, I suppose. Self-pity? Frustration? I can't really say.

Perhaps the shell of a person knows something should be felt and certain actions performed, but there is nothing to connect it to.

Things often feel like that; unattached, nothing to plug things into, just patterns and words. And that's fine, because words mean whatever their use is. Because there are patterns. Infinitely many so.

All is chaos, and people see faces in the clouds. They draw the constellations on the stars and give them names. They draw faces on me and write me a story. That cloud is a dragon. Leo is a lion, brave and strong. Fred is… Fred is whatever I thoughtlessly told him I'd like him to be.

But the words are just words. What they describe is not real. What they say is imaginary. What they show, that's what is real. How things fit together. Where all the best views can be had.

Which buttons do what? And I sometimes think that there is a part of me that may feel grief. Or a shadow of me. Or a shadow of grief. I do not know. Beetle in a box.

I have heard some people say that psychopaths envy self-esteem. This is absurd. What sense would that make? We just re-arrange it.

You can have your self-esteem. It just cannot be higher than mine, which means sometimes there needs to be a bit of reorganization done. So long as you credit me for it; you can be as proud of yourself as you like.

Like a pyramid scheme, really. The wealthier you get, the wealthier I get. As long as I'm the capstone, all is well.

There are only two sins: trying to take my place or failing to support me. Competing with or letting down. Even so, if you want to talk about how beautiful, my reflection of you is, that is fine.

However, when I am manic, I do not merely reflect. I polish; I amplify. You cannot be more confident in yourself than I am in myself at these times. No-one could. As confident? Maybe.

Other people have neurological functions of their own, working within at least broadly the same parameters as mine, so it seems reasonable to assume it.

That is what souls are, mirrors in people, for them to dress up and stand before as their Ideal Me. Whichever one you looked into you'd find the same. Maybe that's how we recognize people as people; we project ourselves onto their behavior and see if it matches up.

Isn't that what emotion is; behavior? We tell how people feel by watching their actions. By that account, the only difference is I don't project back.

The narcissistic side of me likes to hear themselves talk. I can only assume that if 'normal', non-narcissistic people are as I describe them – desperate to live their idealizations – then a narcissistic person is going to behave even more so.

Maybe the mask has two sides, one for outward, one for inward. As I said, reading some of the descriptions at your forum of how people behave in relationships was what I found familiar.

Like most people, until then I thought it was the Bateman and Leather faces of the world. Sherlock – the BBC drama – is just about the only positive media portrayal of psychopaths I'm aware of. I mean... very silly. But at least a step.

We can be very useful, contributive individuals; scientists, philosophers, astronauts, doctors, artists. Different perspectives are so much more valuable than anyone recognizes.

Do you think that only non-narcissistic/psychopathic/sociopathic (I find the last a more comfortable label in many ways. I am not merely vain, and I am not a violent brute, which I know are common-consciousness connotations of the first two. Pride? '

Phantom' sensibilities that never formed properly or died young?) People are aware of the media depictions and prevailing attitudes?

Being gay does not seem 'wrong' to a gay person, but they know that it does to a lot of others because they are immersed in it.

I have been thinking about your question from earlier. I still have moods, if that is what you mean. Maybe it doesn't come across well because you're talking to the ego more directly than usual, and I am trying to stay within The Lines.

Do I have no super-ego or only part of one? It doesn't matter. This is the nature of disorders and definitions.

You – the normal people – decide where the cut-off lines are. I don't.

I think I am naturally free of prejudice. Imagine a world where everyone was free of racism, homophobia, and sexism. There needs to be more of me, not less. And there will be.

When people get caught up doing things, they get lost in them. I am no different. It's just I can also get lost in who I'm currently being asked, begged to be. It is subconscious so often. I just want people to be happy.

Or does the narcissist just not want to take responsibility, hmm?

It strikes me that you may not know what I mean by feeling powerful. Maybe you do. If there were any degree of certainty, we'd not be having the conversation in the first place I suppose. Feeling powerful is exactly like feeling angry. But good. Same set, different lighting.

By now though, I hope that my bombast and melodrama have made their point. It is not intentional. But it doesn't need to be intentional to be dangerous, if it works how I think it does.

And if it isn't intentional, promises, to the contrary, would be meaningless, even if you were so disposed to believe them. But I think the intensity of the last few days has been, in a way, a microcosm of how things go.

I am sad to say that I think it may not be what I have always taken it for, which was passion. Regrettably, I think what it might actually be is more smoke and mirrors. Emotional Shock & Awe, in every sense.

I have been thinking about empathy. The prevailing opinion appears to be that you either have it, or you don't. I think this is reductive. So back to geometry. Imagine empathy is the Necker Cube[14] I linked to. To have the cube, you need all the vertices, and they have to be connected correctly. This cube is empathy.

---

[14] A Necker cube is an optical illusion of a transparent cube where the orientation of the cube appears to alternate.

Some people have no vertices at all for this construct. Others may have the right number but arranged wrongly. Or the wrong number and arranged wrongly. But what if there are some people - like me - who have noticed this 'wrongness' and tried to correct it?

That is what coping strategies and mirroring is all about. So I would reject the idea that it is as simple as you have it, or you don't. There must be degrees of approximation, of similarity. On a good day, I think I can get close. Say 9/12 vertices in the right arrangement. Other days I have something much more akin to a disorganized pile of sticks.

This ties into the narcissist/sociopath point. When I am more manic, I am more the latter. When I am less manic, I revert to merely the former.

I think the people who lack all the vertices are the psychopathic end of the spectrum. But it does seem likely that my approximations do function as emotions for me. The problem is they don't quite 'lock' with the real thing; the key doesn't fit the lock. Then the bullshit starts to maintain the illusion.

If you loved someone and just as you reached what should be intimacy that happens. Instead of running as fast as possible - which is absolutely the sensible thing to do, even in the most extreme of cases (like mine, I hope) - their need to empathize causes them to try to soothe it.

To grab onto it and try to restore order, only to find there was none in the first place. By which point you're spinning through the air, upside-down and watching pigs and bits of the barn whizz past. This is where I think; I go beyond narcissism and engage in bona fide sociopathy. Like the deeper, you go the more obvious the mess is, I suppose.

Fred
I have upset you. My apologies.

Dianne
Why are you asking me if I am upset? It reminds me of someone that I know casually a few times she has made that comment and my reply to her is the same to you. Gee I didn't feel upset, but perhaps you can give me some good reasons, and I can try to be upset.

Fred
The problem with being honest – or as I am actually being, openly speculative – about this sort of thing, is people always look for the other agenda, assuming there must always be one. Also please bear in mind that I am looking at myself in this light only as a form of understanding.

I honestly do have an interest in learning. Perhaps I shall walk away from our exchanges and decide that perhaps it is something else.

This is to say, I contacted you for the reasons I have already given. I haven't contacted others, although it has crossed my mind to do so. However, your site stated research, not just 'support' or 'advice' or whatever.

I imagine if I contacted someone who ran a forum that didn't have this underpinning; they would be considerably more hostile to me.

And, of course, ever-present whim. I thought you might help me find some answers. Obviously, you'd be unlikely to do that in exchange for nothing, so I share my speculation from my perspective.

My thoughts on things. It is barter. Are you finding it unpleasant? I'm trying to be objective about things, which is not really my home turf so to speak, so I probably sound a bit crazy.

Look at it this way: the closer you get to the set, the easier it is to see the windows are painted on. Usually the audience stays in the gallery so this isn't a problem. All the usual coping strategies are not in place.

The reason there is the presumption you will not respond is because after years of experience that is the attitude expected.

Dianne
The reason you may think that I might be upset is that we are in a deep type of conversation in writing. I prefer it that way because I think we can be more open and honest in this method of communicating.

I would think that since you are missing my visual cues, it would be new territory for you.

Fred

Firstly, on my apology for upsetting you. It is very difficult for me to tell. In some ways, to do this I feel a bit like, I have to take what I believe is called a leap of faith. I do not have a problem with lying, but I dislike being lied to. In some ways, you could say I react similarly to most people, only my reaction is one of rising frustration rather than 'hurt'.

The reason for this is that people lying to me is very suspicious. It makes me feel they are trying to take away my control/stability, which obviously; I'm not enthused about happening. Valid reasoning and I'm yet to find a way around it. This leads me to conclude that I need to extend this to myself.

Can I lie to me? If I do, I want to know about it. I want to stop it. I've seen what happens to people who believe their own mythology. Half the time, I am what happens to them.

Obviously, you'd be an idiot to drop your guard, but I am being as honest as I can be.

Do you see how hard it is to try and establish any kind of trust here? Not because I distrust you, not because you distrust me, but because you distrust what I am. Not even who I am; what I am. Not even am! Might be.

There's a basic assumption that because I can, I will. Even though I don't more often than I do. Or is it not that I can, but that I ever would? Is that the invisible line I cross that causes such revulsion?

I am honestly interested in your answer to that. Is that what I don't understand; it is not that I am willing to cross these absurd, invisible lines, but that I do? Even with no lasting damage. No real hurt.

I make mistakes, just like everyone else. They're mine, though. I don't allow anyone else to make them for me. Or do I? Is that the delusion of a narcissist or is it true?

Again, it doesn't matter. I must act in the most rationally advantageous way possible.

It is not that I am untrustworthy; it is that I am incapable of trusting. I'm not sure I understand how I would go about doing so. Maybe that's what people see in the end. Once the show is over.

Maybe that's what the control replaces; the capacity to place trust in others. Maybe not. As far as I know, everyone uses control. They just use invisible rules to do it because they're not capable of confronting it for what it is.

God Said So. No, you just wanted to. And that's okay. They get their imaginary friends to fight for them.

What a stupid game to play. Isn't it obvious that I could just imagine a bigger, stronger imaginary friend? That's the tone, the standard, the metric.

And then they bring an imaginary knife to a gunfight. Not that it would make any difference if they brought a real knife or even a gun, since if they were capable of using either, then they wouldn't need them.

There are dangerous individuals out there who are far viler than I am. Probably, a good sight more than 1% of the population. Maybe as high as 5% if the spectrum is considered in a broader sense.

Some will just cause ruin, but a few will mercilessly kill, steal and destroy just for the sheer fun of it.

I don't want to dress things up and make people think psychopathic people are never a danger. But then, the same could be said of non-psychopathic people, too.

But if I am one in any way, significantly far from the line of best fit that society has drawn through itself, I hope I am proof that we are not all bad, not all intentionally cruel and not all mercilessly self-interested. Moreover, and for obvious reasons,

I hope that if I am, I can become proof that it is not always beyond repair and redemption.

Dianne
I am curious what got you exploring what you might, deep down, be really all about to put a name to it? Was there a moment in time, thing's others said to you?

I guess I am asking what piqued your intellectual curiosity.

Fred

What opened my curiosity was that after trying to solve the same problems the same ways and being dissatisfied with the results, I decided maybe there are better methods, and that it would be worth learning them.

We are all problem-solving machines. Empiricist meat. On this matter, I suppose we could be said to be working on the same problem: me. Only obviously I call it 'everyone else'. There's a truth to both.

When wolves run out of sheep, they go hungry. When sheep run out of wolves, they are free to eat grass. What if I could eat both? What if I could enjoy eating both?

I can't see how it could do anything other than improve things for all parties, even if only incrementally so. Increments add up though. Trust me, I should know.

What is needed is not that I do not take the 'obvious' or 'common sense' choices presented to me, but that another understanding of these things be reached.

Learn something else so well that it develops its own kind of obvious. Find a new kind of sense. I cannot see how it would be a disadvantage. Quite the opposite.

Even in the worst-case scenario I would not stand to lose out. If I were to succeed, I could gain much. Does that not strike you as common sense? I ask because I want to know how wide the chasm really is. In a sense - I can't say if in your sense - I do genuinely want to be able to cross it.

To connect. If nothing else, I think you, guys have all my plug sockets, and apparently it's not cool for me to keep inviting you, over so I can borrow yours.

Is the end result any different for me if I can find some sockets of my own? I think so, but I think it could be better.

Remember: I always want better. Disappointment abounds. Besides, it isn't like I'll forget how to borrow them if it doesn't work out. It isn't necessarily zero-sum though.

I have also said on several occasions that I understand words well. How they work. I particularly like those things, too. Who doesn't? Nobody prefers listening to people they consider stupid over people they consider smart. Its content less tautology that sounds like it tells me something about you whilst also flattering me. It's good!

I like the fact it doesn't specify that I am such an individual of the first type. It sounds like it says that, but it doesn't. Even the flattery is an illusion. It is tofu, not steak. It is also a test.

Let me put it this way: if you are still thinking you will learn anything with 'true or false' here, then you need to rethink. It is why the warnings are always missed. It seems to be a big part of what upsets people so much.

The world is not so neat as to always fall into just two categories. I am 'somewhat sociopathic' in the sense I outlined when I differentiated between people like me and the chainsaws & Ponzi's crowd. Somewhat by degree. Somewhat because it seems you find it helpful to think of me as something half-finished, an improvement. An upgrade. Evolution.

What do you want me to reflect? Poor old me, or Here Be Dragons? No! What did I just explain to you? I can say Here Be Dragons in the way most people say Poor Old Me.

That's the whole scam, boiled down. That should have read "rather than an improvement. An upgrade. Evolution." This is what happens when I allow myself to be distracted by silly little girls. Do not worry, I am now focused again.

Dianne
You seem to be quite intelligent, and certainly articulate. Does that make it easier or harder to think about your differences from others?

Fred
I probably am smarter than most. Do you really think that or are you feeding the ego to fuel the mouth? Perhaps I should stop saying anything at all, to check. Either way, that doesn't mean I am infallible.

I am also impulsive and enjoy talking about myself. These are short-term gains that do not guarantee a longer-term benefit of greater magnitude than you stand to see.

I am pleased that you consider me very high functioning and not just for the obvious ego reasons. If that's what I am, then I do not wish to be it, did not ask to be it and it does not make me any less motivated to be a good person.

If anything, it would probably make me more so. However, I think if I am very high functioning now and some sort of British middle class sociopath, perhaps this gives me a better chance of finding/developing conceptual structures, coping mechanisms and socio-emotional proxies to further compensate for... any miscibility.

I think it would be fair to say I have an abiding hatred for avoidable imperfections. Maybe unavoidable ones, too.

I suppose this could be where my self-perception lets me down, and really I don't come across like that at all (which would be a bit crappy, since I'm being myself as hard as I can be to do this properly).

I suppose I may also ask as an example of the sort of question that I feel should be asked of ourselves. "Is my own subconscious interfering with my judgment?" as it were? I think like this all the time, so I suppose you could say I don't even trust myself.

It's about as much fun as it must sound. I do not mean anything by asking and really hope it doesn't come across as rude or patronizing.

However, it crossed my mind and bothered me enough that I felt compelled to ask it and you're simply flattering me with comments regarding high-functioning status. Maybe a lot of things. It just bears thinking about such things.

I also like observing things. I'm guessing that there are probably some distinctive patterns to how a sociopath communicates, such as using depersonalized/objectifying terms in place of 2nd/3rd person pronouns or talking around a subject in what seems like circles.

The latter would be an example of looping, which I suspect is one of the more common and ingrained behaviors; I've noticed fitting into the picture.

As you say, we are all different. I cannot say for sure I feel compassion in the way you do. I think I do, but probably not identically. It is something that fascinates me, to the extent that I have written something on the subject.

I understand it; compassion is the antithesis of efficiency. If you want to do something as efficiently as you can, you cannot also do it compassionately.

Compassion is in part taking the extra time to do something inefficiently because it is good to do it that way, not because it is easiest or quickest. I think I'm fairly certain on that. I understand it.

I try to practice it, too. Probably not that well, which annoys me, but I have at least a rough idea of how it works.

The thing is, it is true. I am not just saying it, but have a feeling attached. Is that feeling the same as yours is? Clearly, I cannot say. Is it what I "pin" compassionate behavior and feelings on? Sure. The two are the same for me; the meaning of a feeling is what situations the feeling occurs in.

Sometimes I experience compassionate feelings. Sometimes I feel loving ones. Other times, I feel angry or depressed or rejected ones. Is that not what life is?

My own experiences may differ in some ways from yours, internally/emotionally speaking, but that does not mean that I do not have them or give them labels. I just seem to be less controlled by them.

If I make a 'bad' decision, I get over it more quickly because I accept that these things happen. Why beat myself up over inevitable imperfections when I'm doing such a good job on other imperfections?

I make them less often than others, which makes me better than them at it. If there were any doubt, then why is there a pathological hatred of me but none for people who are just plain stupid?

I'm not going to lie, Dianne; this is a real can of worms. I won't try to pin the blame on you alone, but you at least helped me open it. Can I close it? If I can't, what the hell am I supposed to do with all these worms? WHO OR WHAT AM I?

This is fucking ridiculous. My brain is in tatters, and I want to reconstruct it, but it looks more and more like it is a choice between "be yourself and destroy everything you ever 'cared' about" and "never be yourself and bask in the shadows of happiness."

I don't know happiness, Dianne. I really don't think I do. Yet it is what the rest of the world expects, demands AND hopes of me. Sometimes I think it'd just be tidier if I killed myself and saved suffering on both sides of the fence.

I'm too clever and they are too stupid. Being strong is tiresome when you get nothing but insanity and weakness in return.

Dianne
It sounds as if you are feeling a bit depressed when you think about your life to date.

Fred
I was born. It took me several years to learn the world. Now I'm just really disappointed in it. Worst of all, I'm really disappointed in my failure to change it or even see a future worth saving.

I'm among the best and the brightest, and I'm so terminally broken and alienated that I will never, ever be accepted.

Let us all burn. Let me burn. Let me burn now. I'm more rational than nearly everyone; I'm more intelligent and, despite an innate inability to even make sense of most of it; I'm still a better person than most on moral grounds.

This is a sick joke, and I am not laughing. I think, perhaps; it is time to leave. I'm not depressed, but if there is no prospect of happiness and every prospect of disaster and pain, why continue? Tell me. Why do people get up? Why do they go to bed? What the hell is the point if you can't be yourself, living in the pursuit of happiness?

This isn't something I asked for. It isn't something I wantonly abuse. It's just who I am, and if I told most of the people, I care about, they would no longer care about me. I was damned before I was born, and people blame me for even being alive. Good-bye redemption, hello... whatever this is. So maybe it's time to say good-bye to that as well.

And you know what? If I left a note explaining who I am, what I am and what it means, not even my nearest and dearest would mourn my passing.

And maybe that is the truth of it; a sociopath is their own first victim and the one who rarely if ever has a chance to get out.

Perhaps that is why I sought out a support forum for victims, not somewhere full of braggarts who would enable my own less desirable traits.

I hope I'm lucky enough to escape the nurture, to undo it. I also hope I'm lucky enough to take real control, to be freed somewhat from the nature side of things. Ironically, maybe to relinquish control over certain areas of my life and redirect them to other areas, where it is more needed and will be put to a better use.

Part of this means getting some perspective of my own talents, skill-sets and the extent of my personal agency. Am I really a good writer? I shall have to find out against the only benchmark, there is; trying to become a professional writer.

Am I really a kind person? If I behave in kind ways, then I guess I will be by definition. But also, if I am not solely to blame for all this, if the buyers should have stopped to check the product and are partly victims of their own greed, do I really have to blame myself for that?

It now strikes me as arrogant to think that I am so powerful and clever and devious and charming that it was ever all me. I am taking credit for other people's failings, which means I am also carrying the burden of blame for them.

Narcissism is a character defect, and I suppose if I am now stuck being fully self-aware of my actions and tendencies, the narcissist within me agrees with me that I need to improve on this.

Trying to cover it up hasn't helped at all, so why not shoot for the stars and try to become the one (first one? If I think hard and am honest, I doubt it.

But it can't be all that common, at least) who inverts the whole disorder into a real strength, genuine improvement and success. Not fake and fragile and in constant need of protection when it comes under too-close scrutiny.

I think I can be honest enough to counter the narcissism, and I am intelligent enough to solve the sociopathic side of things. I don't think that is self-delusion. If anything, it is more an observation of a process that has already started.

I did say that your forum is important because it helps people when they really need it, didn't I? That it lets them move on and escape the control of a sociopath. It may even be able to do that when the sociopath in question not only got into your head but IS your head.

I think - with time, at least - I may be living proof of that. I very nearly wasn't. And I know how I shall repay you, too; by passing on the kindness and support to others in need. I hope this is acceptable, but it seemed like the kind of repayment you would like most of all.

Besides, isn't the whole subtext of this that I find myself the most fascinating puzzle of them all?

But I'm thinking clearly and more sanely than in... too many years I think, if I'm honest. I think this clarity can help me, and it can help other people too. I can help other people too. People like me and people who have had the unfortunate experience of run-ins with people like me.

When you have a disease of thought - which I guess is what this sort of thing really is, whatever its cause - then surely the cure must come in the form of ideas?

Reshape the thought process to cure the disease. I know it isn't curing cancer, but it's worth finding out, isn't it? I don't expect miracles, but perhaps it could improve the lives of people on both sides of it all. I do not need chemicals; I need better thoughts. I need to connect those thoughts to actions.

Dianne
Do you ever wish you were a "normal" person?

Fred
I am just different. Imagine two people wanted to play draughts (checkers; I believe you guys call it) but only had a chess set. They agree to use the pieces as proxies for the draughts themselves. You walk in and see them doing that and think "that is not how you play chess." That is all this is.

It seems to have the unfortunate side effect of sending people into a spin, though. My reality is so like your reality that at first it looks the same. But it is not. There are crooked pictures everywhere.

I think I am normal. Other people think they are normal. There are more of them than there are of me, so they decide, which is and, which isn't. I'm a standard deviation or two or five or however, many it takes to be the wrong side of the line that other people drew saying, "this is it, go no further or be banished."

You use your strength in numbers. I use my own strengths. Not to push back, but to glide on through. Isn't this a battle of ideas? What Works Best.

Without meaning to sound rude, I think that if you think, a sociopath would prefer to be anything but a sociopath, you may be missing part of what makes them such. I don't have any wish to be anything other than myself.

Would I prefer that self to be one without an inherent darkness and propensity to damage others? Well sure, but there are many reasons for wishing that, and I suspect that most people would want to be less like that, so it doesn't tell us much. Who doesn't want to be a 'better' person?

If the difference is going to be pinned down beyond neurological and genetic - which is to say, if it is to be definitional behavioral in some respect - then we surely must consider how this drive differs from the norm in people with psychopathy.

Everyone differs, in particular, neurological and genetic traits, as this is what makes us individuals rather than some dispersed gestalt entity that acts in unison in all things. What we are concerned with - and by - is how this translates into interpersonal behavior.

Is my desire to be a better person qualitatively different from yours or anyone else's?

I suppose the short version of that is; does it matter if the motivator towards self-improvement and the foundation for social action are rational or emotional?

Not, are they identical, but are they necessarily different in terms of results? It seems to me that they are not, and that they are both different methods that can lead to the same conclusions. Good or bad.

For lack of a better word? Let's call a spade a spade here; it's arrogance.

Rationalizing in the above way is something I'm very good at. It has been used to justify actions to myself, to excuse previous actions and so forth. That is part of what I am turning on its head, by using the same reasoning and analytic skills to be more intensely critical of myself and my actions.

That doesn't mean that those criticisms are of things that have necessarily been done with conscious intent (although a few are, such as the couple's counseling thing), as in many cases - a significant majority of them - they were done purely out of reflex and with good intent.

Or at least without bad intent. I am not a malicious or cruel person, whatever you think.

I have various theories, but in a broad sense they boil down to "the meaning of linguistic acts is tied to shared experience of the world and if two people have substantially different experiences, then this is a major obstacle to clear communication."

It would be like trying to describe colors to someone who has never seen, or imagining a completely new color that isn't a composite or shade of an existing one. The question is which side of the equation is the blind one in this instance?

I actually think the only honest answer to that is 'both'; there are things you 'see' in the world that I do not and there are things that I 'see' that you do not.

In a sense, we live in subtly but irreconcilably different worlds. There is so much beauty and wonder and insight that I wish I could discuss, share, examine and celebrate. A lot of it is essentially inexpressible in the senses that I wish to convey.

Similarly, there seem to be points of deeply held value, a kind of instinctive discourse that many people are able to engage in, that I just don't seem to be able to understand. Not 'cannot make sense of', but 'cannot make sense of in the way others do'.

We are each incapable of ever fully bridging that divide. You are too mired in your own perspectives to be able to step outside them and see them for what they are.

I am too incapable of ever attaching to a given perspective enough to give up all the others, which is what I would need to do in order to understand what it is to truly hold it to be true.

I may be able to see the acts for what they are, but that renders me incapable of knowing what it would be like to sincerely hold them in the way people apparently do. Which is not to say I cannot be sincere or that nothing matters to me, because that would be very far from the truth indeed.

It is not so much that I am unwilling to entertain a new concept, but that I am not talking with you how I would with most people. I'd expect to be considered a rambling madman if I were like this all the time, as it's very much a case of trying to express things in the gaps between the words, to illustrate something that there's no common terminology for me to simply describe it with.

Hence using what other people would say; their words for their games. Mine do not translate well, even when meant kindly. Which they usually are. I don't expect you to believe that, but they are. It's complicated.

I am probably passively more confrontational than is normal and without seeing it as confrontation. This may be down to my not having any deep attachment to most of my positions or beliefs, whereas most people seem to. I explore ideas without pretense, which includes the more day-to-day civilities that many people seem to value bafflingly highly.

With the wording, I'm a very tangential thinker. Too tangential, to the point of it being a problem, particularly when I'm being introspective. I like to connect things up, find patterns, and learn new things through exploring ideas and so on.

There's no intent to misdirect and when I want to be, I can be very to the point. In person, I will often contribute more along the lines of interjections, witty comments and so forth.

In my communication with you, I've been the most serious I ever have, as ordinarily, I take very few things so seriously that I won't joke about them, often self-deprecatingly.

As I believe I've said, you're talking more to a sort of disassociated, self-reflective 'version' of me. That isn't to say more real, because there is no doubt in my mind that the me that I am most of the time around my family, and close friends is very much the 'real' me. Although that's oversimplifying something astonishingly complex, whoever says it.

With regard to your honesty, I'm interested to know how you'd account for a few things. Firstly, I do care very much about various things that are not purely self-interested. I've not been joking when I say morality concerns me deeply, for example.

There's a very fine balancing act between removing myself to maintain objectivity and switching off completely, which tends to lead to a super-analytic remoteness. Not only does that upset other people but, after the fact, I have to admit that it unsettles me a bit as well.

I'd describe it as like being able to switch your vision to monochrome so you can better track movement without being distracted - or overwhelmed - by all the pretty colors you usually see. All the vivacity and meaning vanishes, but I'm better able to focus on the job at hand.

I used to think it was purely a talent, but to an extent, it is also a bit of a curse, because the complete shut-down removes so much context that I end up unable to function properly; I'm living in too different a world to everyone else to make properly sound decisions.

Maintaining the balance can be quite a drain though, particularly as my instincts can sometimes be screaming to either let go and go into glorious, chaotic free-fall or switch off completely and for good as a kind of safety mechanism.

CHAPTER FOUR
Gaslighting
Control through Manipulation

"Gaslighting is a form of mental abuse in which information is twisted/spun, selectively omitted to favor the abuser, or false information is presented with the intent of making victims doubt their own memory, perception and sanity"
— Wikipedia

Dianne
Many people comment that psychopaths are manipulative and play "head games" to control their victims. Do you manipulate people?

Steve
I found that there is a condition that some people get that makes them perfect to be handled by people. I found it as I was looking for things that I could tell people to hide my behaviors.

Dianne
What kind of things do you need to hide?

Steve
It was just about the games I play. I was only saying that I tend to play those games to get a change in a person or to make them more dependent on me, so I have more control.

Dianne
What kind of games do you play?

Steve
There are many games you can play to make people think things that you want, like the damaged card, but here's one off the top of my head.

I would tell my girl to meet me at a bar for a drink, and before she gets there I go and find a staff member that I think she will be jealous of and start talking to them, but in a way that will not make them think I was trying to pick them up, but so they seem familiar.

Maybe even tell them you're meeting your girl there, and it's a really nice place. But keep an eye out for her to walk in so you see her first.

Then you can pretend you didn't see her come in and before she comes over to you can say something funny to get the staff member to giggle a bit and then go to walk off.

Then your girl has seen you with them and is not sure what to think and when she asks who was that, thinking that you might be friends you just say "no one" or "just an old friend."

Don't offer to introduce them. That's just a small game to play, is that what you meant?

Fred
People play games and when certain moves are made, other counter-moves are much more likely to follow. It follows that if your appearance is a move and therefore, triggers certain probable responses; you can predict those responses and make better use of them.

Everything is about appearances. Possibly not the best bit of reinforcement for you there, but it's true. Turn up to work looking like a tramp, and they will try to fire you. Turn up at the disciplinary hearing wearing a smile and a suit, and they'll apologize and give you money.

The problem for many is that they attach deep meaning to these patterns, their neurological response mechanisms become shaped by them, and they come to think of them as 'right' or 'good'. They are neither, merely useful.

Press's green to punch, red to jump and blue to roll in wasted at 8am the day of some partner's friend's wedding and fire off a few salvos of "you're unreasonable, needy and pitiful to even suspect my motives, I was up all night with a distressed friend" when asked for an explanation.

Without thinking. As a matter of course. It is natural and easiest.

Maybe saying we are playing a different game is misleading: we are all playing the same game, but only some of us are aware of it.

Dianne
How do these games help you control someone? Do you have any particular words or ways that you can effectively make them think it is their fault?

Steve
It's easy to make someone think things are their fault; you just have to make them doubt themselves, which is easier when they have low

self-esteem. Like if I said, "You have a brain like a sieve," then changed a few things around on you without you knowing, like times and appointments you made and where your phone and keys are.

Then you would start to believe that I was right after a while. Then I blame you for forgetting something, and you would just think it was you and say sorry.

Dianne
The example you give when explaining games is helpful because that helps give some context to what games mean to you.

That said if you would like to add any more examples that would be useful as I am guessing you have quite a few games, both subtle and more direct that you have found work well for you.

What are some specific examples of the damaged card that you play? I assume you are also saying there is a problem if you make up a story about being damaged, and then it can get confusing to keep track of the details?

Or do you isolate your partners from people who know you well so the stories won't conflict?

Steve
Damaged Card. You need to be careful if you do this too early; it needs to be something that you tell them about yourself that no one else knows,

and it needs to be something that it's not normal for everyone to know like:

    Hearing voices (but just one).
    Being molested when young.
    Watching a close friend commit suicide.
    Being bashed by your parents at a young age.
    Having severe depression.
    And one that does work.
    It surprisingly is Remorseful Ex-Hit Man.

Dianne
I had to chuckle over the hit man card used, personally that would make me run, but it is interesting that it works so well.

I can picture you adding some mystery by saying that you would be able to tell them only a tiny bit.

If they got curious about this moment, you could go silent and say, I can't talk about it because I want to protect you from my past.

Does it go something like that?

Steve
Yes, that's pretty much how it goes but its good because that's not something that people tell each other, so she will just tell her friends that you have a dark past.

Dianne
The term "gaslighting" explains what you do as far as telling them their mind is like a sieve and then proceeding to trick them over things.

Or planting information in their heads.

Bill
You hit the hypothetical nail on the head with your comment about planting information. This is my golden goose. As for gaslighting, I honestly have never heard the term. I had to look it up. After reading the definition, I would say it is a tool I use daily. It is amazing to me how mold-able memory really is.

If you trust me enough, and I'm convincing enough, you will remember an event as I told you it happened. You will defend my version as the absolute truth.

Even better, you will be outraged at the injustice that even put me under and rise to my defense. This coupled with ideas planted around, and I am now in the position to become the hero.

I can save the agency from the looming disaster that no one saw coming. Better yet, I can save the agency from the looming disaster that the guy in the office I want is causing.

Fred
Gaslight is a term I have only just learned, but I like it very much. The term, that is. It suits what it is perfectly. Not just intent, but spectacle.

Make them flicker, make them dim, make them blaze brighter than ever before, push the limits of brightness and darkness without ever overstepping and turning them off or burning them out.

Don't you want to burn brightly? I do. We're more alive at the edge. Hah. Some of us are only alive at the edge. Or over it. Falling, forever. I think it might tie-in with the word salad concept. I don't really go in for that myself, because why talk nonsense when you can get something more constructive done with sense?

Anyway, it is yet more misdirection, stalling for thinking time, muddying the waters. But word salad is basically gaslighting a conversation by wobbling the other person's brain around with so many mad jumps, non sequiturs and juxtapositions that they can only assume, they're being stupid.

Frankly, most people are so confused be a coherent, true account delivered at speed and with details that talking nonsense seems like a waste of time.

Dianne
Do you have more examples of gaslighting?

Fred
My favored alternative to sounding like a babbling loon (I hope I don't, anyway!) is to give something such an incredibly detailed on-the-fly analysis that it's a bit like reaching a deadline only to realize you've done none of the work.

The catching up never quite does catch up though, so the other person is always a few steps behind and unclear on why.

What does this achieve? Self-doubt. Am I following him properly? Is he right and I'm actually not quite smart enough to keep up with him in full flow? Have I made a massive blunder?

Half the time, people take themselves from here straight to being on the defensive and don't really know why. Whilst knowing I've just explained why to them and am patiently trying to go over it again for the slower kids at the back of the class.

Is the person who apparently knows what is going on more or less likely than the increasingly confused, slightly upset person who doesn't? Context is set; the framework of the conversation now contains a few innocuous assumptions that you haven't even noticed creeping in...

And the grass doesn't get mowed, or I go to sleep off my hangover without further questioning or whatever it was that I had suddenly found myself having to problem-solve without preparation.

I'm sure you'll have come across it before, but heavily implying but straight-faced-denying there are other women sniffing around is another one. As I said before, people are much more likely to act conservatively than they are speculatively.

Women all seem to utterly despise each other anyway, so a little reminder that I'm with them out of choice rather than necessity can help keep things peaceful.

Mostly, this keeps the other, even more insane neuroses at bay. Like debt consolidation for anxieties, I suppose. Similarly, not showing any interest or concern when the other person goes out with a male friend seems to give much the same results.

If (or rather, when it is brought up. It will be. Without fail. Especially if they're doing it to try to get a rise out of me because, then who is the mega-bitch? And it backfires in their face) it is then brought up; the response is "I'm not crippled by insecurities and don't have an overwhelming need to control you.

If you could try offering me the same degree of confidence and respect, then maybe we'd not have so many arguments over imagined slights."

On the other hand, perhaps I am just unusual in that I'm not pre-meditatively malicious about it. I suppose the fact that I can go from exploding with rage one minute to totally serene and conciliatory the next is probably the 'main' form. Or vice versa.

Loudly explaining that I'm not getting involved, it is a waste of my time to discuss it with someone so reasonable, that I am going out, all while very clearly doing the opposite of these things is probably another.

Completely unemotional disinterest followed by apparently frantic emotional pleas or extreme anger, upset or seeming confusion would be another.

Dianne
What makes it easy to isolate your girlfriends from their friends? Do you have to tell them you don't like the friends

or what would be an example of how you would get them to give up on their friends?

Steve
This is something I do to get them to become dependent on me to make the power in the relationship shift to my side. It's easy to isolate them from their friends, but family can take longer, and I don't think I would do that if it is not going to last more than three years.

Fred
With regard to isolation, we're back in the territory of my analyzing my own behavior under a particular understanding. I do not set out to isolate people.

I'm not even sure if I do it, particularly at all, but rather tend to end up with people who are already isolated.

My absolutely honest answer in terms of intent at the time is to 'help' them (patronizing; I realize) or just generally make them happy.

However, the intensity with which my relationships tend to start (and continue and end with... I do not relish the experience of considering and having to admit such things, I must say) means isolation is kind of the order of the day.

At least, unless I meet someone who invites other people on dates or to bed with us, which I think I'd find pretty weird. They'd certainly need to be very attractive, put it that way!

Dianne
How do you go about isolating them from their friends?

Steve
This is easy – make the friend flirt with you in front of them or sabotage something in her life that would benefit the friend and sow doubt about their friendship being one sided.

Dianne
Some members of my forum have mentioned that their sleep has been disrupted. Is this a technique you use?

Fred
I don't deliberately disturb sleep patterns, but I also make little effort to alter mine to be less disruptive. Sometimes I'll barely sleep for days or weeks, other times I'll be overwhelmed with sloth.

Thinking about it, this does rarely coincide with known plans of my partner, and any conflict is likely to be addressed in a similar fashion to the lawn-mowing example.

Also, I don't know if it counts, but sometimes when I'm particularly frustrated I'll land a really precise blow to an emotional weak spot, but do it in an apparently oblivious way; "you're unfit for motherhood," "you're incapable of relaxing," "this is why you don't have any friends."

These can all be entirely true, but they sort of slip out in very calculated, rational tones and therefore, don't sound like they've been said purely out of anger.

I will then later claim that they were said purely out of anger, but perhaps drop in a "but there's some truth to it, I suppose" because nobody likes a back-tracker.

Steve
Changing people's sleep patterns helps to create a suggestible personality, e.g. keeping them tired by waking them with a clap or a bang on the wall. If they're asleep enough, then they will not know why they woke up, just that they did.

Alternatively, giving people antidepressants or mood stabilizers when they don't need them can mess with the way they think and throw them off balance in a mental sense, and it's not hard to get them nowadays.

Dianne
That is quite clever to use anti-depressants and mood stabilizers, not sure how that would work, do you have to slip them into something and about how long does it take to start to rattle them?

Steve
If I drug someone, it takes three weeks to have a noticeable effect because it is a small dose, and I can cook so it's easy to hide the taste.

The best part is if her friends don't like you, then you can say to them you're worried about her because she's been acting strange and get points with them for being concerned.

Dianne
Why do you think gaslighting works?

Bill

Joseph Goebbels[15] once said, "If you tell a lie big enough and keep repeating it, people will eventually come to believe it. The lie can be maintained only for such time as the state can shield the people from the political, and/or military consequences of the lie.

It becomes vitally important for the state to use all of its power to repress dissent, for the truth is the mortal enemy of the lie, and thus by extension, the truth is the greatest enemy of the state."

Substitute the word "psychopath" for the word "state" and you have the basis for the psychopath's methodology. This is the basis of "gaslighting" technique.

The lie needs to remain fresh in the minds of the ones you are targeting. The liar must keep the target's focus on believing the new reality and not permit them to begin questioning its' authenticity.

This is absolutely crucial; however, it is instinctual for me. I don't, on a conscious level, realize I'm even doing it. For example, if someone swings at you, you flinch. You didn't plan to flinch.

You didn't even know you did it until after you have already flinched. The same is true with me. I don't, at least now always, realizing I'm setting the stage for a lie until after I have already started to do it.

---

[15] Joseph Goebbels was a German politician and Reich Minister of Propaganda in Nazi Germany from 1933 to 1945.

If an opportunity to benefit arises, I instinctually take action to ensure I receive that benefit. I would say it is a rare case that I miss such an opportunity.

Dianne
What is the process of gaslighting that you follow? How does it begin?

Fred
I would think of the starting phase as "falling in love" or "getting to know each other." Gaslighting comes when cracks start to show in these, as a reaction to the threat, they pose.

After a while, this then fades into the getting them to leave phase.

It isn't planned, but it is a depressingly accurate description of at least most of my relationships. I do remember when I was younger and still in education, a girlfriend left me rather unexpectedly.

I would make a point of holding quiet conversations with other people in the same room as her, but constantly glancing over as if not wanting to be overheard and then ending on a joke so myself and whoever I was talking to would laugh.

Obviously, she thought we were laughing at her, which would sometimes be compounded by the fact I'd draw their attention to her as the reason for my having to go, so they would glance over too.

I'd be talking about an assignment or just plain old shooting the breeze, but make it look like something else.

The best bit? When the other people were challenged by her on this, wanting to know what I had been saying, they would completely deny any knowledge and tell her to stop being so paranoid.

Suddenly, it isn't me; it's a conspiracy involving everyone. Without my ever having said a word out of place.

I was pretty vicious back then; I think. Put it down to inexperience and hormonal confusion.

In terms of bond-building, I take a direct approach; tell them that I have trust issues because of something unspecific in my past that led to me having to protect a part of myself against further harm. In a way, it is kind of true!

Whatever the truth status of it, the outcome is that they're determined to save me. By which I mean they sell themselves on the idea of being the one who is so wonderful that I open up, let them in and eventually am fixed, when no other woman could do that.

I warn them there's a troubled kind of madness or a dark secret I can't forgive myself for (which then later may turn out to be me being so sensitive and caring that I've spent my life beating myself up over something that wasn't even my fault) or whatever.

I will often state sadly that I know they will one day leave me because everyone always does. Which is also true.

See how the truth encourages people to lie to themselves?

Also, I'm very non-judgmental, patient, forgiving, understanding and able to offer a lot of insight. Those are things people want to encourage, so they send out feelers to test the water; will he accept me for X or Y?

Whatever their greatest insecurity is, they want to assuage it, to put it aside and dive straight in. Want want want. Stroke the lion, tame it, and show your kinship and mastery and poise. Then cry like a baby when you get scratched or bitten.

People trust me because they want to trust me. I want them to trust me. I even want to be able to trust them. I think it may be the process of realizing yet again that I cannot, and then this starts the decline into disappointment and eventual heartbreak.

Before the relationship evolves to gaslighting, there is the phase where the partner is being reeled in.

From what I understand the goal, here is to get them to first tell everything about themselves and be the great listener you can use later and then when it is your turn to present the image of being a victim of life and saying things to elicit sympathy(?) or bonding?

Maybe things like a rough childhood, some possible sexual abuse, you know those types of things that get shared as a secret to not only keep them from telling others but to draw them into the confidence.

We engineer situations where how people will behave is obvious. Then we fail to behave in this way, forcing the other person to do so. You were over to watch a film and kissed me? But you have a boyfriend! Welcome across the line. The Fun Starts Here.

Dianne
I think I should share what my reactions are to some of your comments. Actually, it is quite surprising to me.

I have only heard gaslighting described by the victim reciting what they felt like it was and really not as much about it as I would have expected. If done well, I think it must be effective because people probably have no clue, and I guess that is the best outcome from your standpoint.

It is so clear when described but so subtle to the person on the receiving end that you can do it over and over without being caught.

I sometimes get a sort of gasp and nervous chuckle. I know it isn't because I would find it funny that people are being hurt or emotionally tortured.

I need some time to process, but initially, I think perhaps there is such coldness to the skill of doing it.

Fred
Perhaps what makes you laugh is the simplicity of it or the psychological insights it gives about how individuals function "Ah! Is that really how people work? Is it that simple? My, oh my, what a world!"

There is a kind of darkly elegant statement to it, too; you think "me" is distinct from "everything else" and your mind is some secret internal control room from which you direct things, but this is not the case at all.

What it does is press on the external mentality of the individual in such a way as saying, "okay, look; you aren't as clever, as subtle or as in touch with reality as you think you are. So don't speak to me like I'm an idiot when you're the one who hasn't given this any real thought." That's hitting the buttons that most people think they've got well hidden, usually even from themselves.

Why does the toilet roll thing bother someone? Because they have a pathological need to impose structure on their surroundings, to operate according to reliable rules. Highlighting this shows the cracks in their self-deception.

Dianne
One person that I am interviewing takes it an extra step and gives his partners anti-depressants or mood stabilizers which he says, and I agree with are easy to get. He

gives them doses as part of the destabilizing process.

I think the entire thing circles back to a need to control or method of controlling to fit the need. What do you think?

Bill

I would not resort to controlling someone through medication. It's not about fairness; I have no delusions what I do is fair. It's about necessity. I don't need medication in order to obtain the results I want.

I want control, but I want full control. I don't want control over a medicated zombie. Might as well just buy another dog.

My first thought, after reading the story, was that he must not have been capable of controlling the subject without chemicals. That's unfortunate. Do I think it is fair game? I suppose.

I guess for those less gifted than myself, must find some other way. I would prefer that particular person be erased from the gene pool.

Simply because, he is inferior. Psychopathy can be a gift; his kind tarnishes that gift for future generations.

I prefer to have my targets willing, although misinformed, cooperation and submission. If that makes sense.

Fred
I have to say that I can't approve of the comments by the other person you mention. I would never, ever medicate someone in such a way and consider it wanton cruelty to do such.

If I'm backed into a corner, then I may well be unpleasant, but systemic manipulation of someone's brain chemistry is pretty disgraceful behavior, and even I can see that.

It's also cheating, basically, like you're saying, "I can't manage to do this on my own merits." Hah!

Performance-enhancing drugs. Pathetic in the extreme.

However, I want to repeat again that this is not my modus operandi at all, and I'd be likely to take action of my own against anyone I discovered to be doing that to someone.

In a sense, I suppose I have to concede to having a god complex of sorts. I don't know at this point whether you'll be surprised by this or not, but the most angry and ruthless I get is when I'm in a state of moral outrage; this is wrong and I shall NOT let it go uncorrected!

Maybe I take it as more of a personal affront than others, but I do have a very strong sense of right and wrong. Which is quite different from saying I'm very good at only behaving in the good ways, because if this process has taught me anything, then it's that apparently I'm not. At least in relationships, even when I'm trying to be.

Dianne

One thing I didn't mention or didn't make clear is that I very, very rarely have such a gasp then laugh type of reaction. Something has to be pretty out there for me to have that kind of a reaction.

I can only think of a couple of times in the last year, and one time was when I was watching Breaking Bad they did something really outrageous that elicited the gasp without the laugh.

So the laugh and gasp are rare for me. To me and a couple of friends that I asked, there was ZERO delight in the nervous laugh but a response to something extreme to absorb and take in.

Fred

I understand the kind of laughter you mean. Would it surprise you that I quite often react similarly? I wouldn't necessarily describe my own as nervous, but surprised, and... I suppose a kind of delight, but in the unexpected discovery sense, not 'raw pleasure'.

I suppose I see people saying/doing things completely outside of how people are expected to act as a kind of connection, that we're not all so totally alien and unalike after all.

I cannot recall whether I reacted at all that way when you related the incident to me, but it wouldn't be out of the question that I did.

Dianne
I am reading that you are thinking you had more of a discovery of something with a laugh of delight. I would think that more the case based on what you said after the "that's deplorable comment?

Fred
I'm not sure what you mean about the discovery of something with the laugh of delight; could you expand on this, please? What I was trying to say was that the fact a social rule, a norm has been broken surprises me, because it is people acting outside of the parameters within which they tend to stay.

Like so not everyone is really so blinded by social conditioning. Some of them can see deeper truths, if that makes sense.

Dianne
Frankly, I am not a person who likes to engage in circular conversations that keep spinning.

I am not going to spend any time finding more examples for you because the one I brought up has turned into a marathon of words and deflection from the original point.

Fred
I am sorry if it has seemed like I am not interested in your reactions and thoughts, as that is not the case. What I was finding frustrating is that my intentions and the degree to which I do or don't assign value seemed to be being misjudged. I don't

dispute that many people would not think to comment on the things I did and whatever I am.

I know I think differently about many things than most people do.

This may have been especially frustrating because I'm trying to be entirely honest about everything. I do realize that my somewhat free-wheeling introspective style throughout a lot of this is not the easiest to understand, so I am not trying to place the blame on you in any way here. However, I did feel concerned that the 'balance' of my comments were being taken very wide of an accurate portrayal.

I agree that it is deplorable on its own grounds, just as I'm sure we agree that murder, rape; domestic violence and so on are all deplorable 'as is'.

In fact, I think all moral positions are necessarily reducible to expressions of a commitment to a value and at the most fundamental level 'just are'.

There can be discussions around why we feel they just are - consent, self-ownership, exploiting power imbalances and so forth - which can be interesting and useful to consider. However, at each step of justification we can always still as "but why X?" (X = the current 'level' of justification), so eventually we must just accept that there is a 'because it just is' underlying it all.

It is similar to when someone views a painting and when asked why they like it, gives all sorts of reasons; it reminds me of my childhood. I like the play of light on shadow. It speaks to me of serenity and all this sort of thing. Really, though, these are observations of psychological self-analysis, a way of constructing a narrative that explains the experience of liking the painting.

At base, the real answer to "why do you enjoy looking at that painting?" is "it gives me pleasure." With morality, it gives a sense of ethical displeasure.
How we explain and justify that to ourselves doesn't change the fact that we did indeed have that experience of the thing rather than a different experience.

Which, I suspect, sounds like a deflection or a tangent. It is not.

How you describe the difference is actually very perceptive, because I suppose that is at least partly what I do. It is also very much what I do when I'm trying to be empathetic.

I suppose you could say that it isn't a case of my not having emotional content - I most certainly do and often quite pronounced; hence bipolar, I suppose - but that it doesn't necessarily connect up to the rational side of my thoughts.

Instead of being struck by the significance and immediacy of the emotive, it plays out while the rational continues uninterrupted, problem-solving and analyzing.

Part of the more impulsive, hedonistic streak is without a doubt a way of trying to block out the constant rushing of analysis and introspection.

Which now I have written it down and thought about, I think is something nearing profound, as insights go; I have to suppress the rational in order to more directly experience the emotional.

It would also go some way to explaining why I'm a much nicer person when I've had a few drinks than I am when I'm sober.

Anyway, back to my point about your description of the difference. I quite agree, and I think you've put your finger on something significant here; it is all about perspectives, puzzles, and truths. The latter being the one I've probably conveyed least coherently, as it is a case of finding the different truths in a situation.

Why is it morally repulsive to do that? Because it is cruel, violates consent, exploits an imbalance in power-relations and so forth. But also because it is just morally ugly. That isn't the only truth though, as even on its own terms it is a bad decision; the emotional and rational aspects, even considered individually, both lead to the same conclusion.

Therefore, it is morally and intellectually wrong. Neither provides a basis by which it is true to say, "this is a good decision," even if you strip it back to raw self-interest and forget how others may feel about it.

So in a way, you've worked out for yourself one of the lessons that people usually falter over in school; just because something seems like a totally alien/unreasonable/pointless perspective that does not mean it is irrational. By extension, there is more to be learned from coming to understand that perspective than there ever is in dismissing it because of emotional reactions.

People do some truly horrible things for emotional reasons, so I'd say most if not all people need to learn to do this much more. Not necessarily then act upon the new understanding, but at least grasp its form and function.

It sounds like your reaction to my examples was similar to how I felt about the anti-depressant example you gave. That's really pretty deplorable.

It's also profoundly stupid, because it is leaving a chemical trail that will be picked up if the person goes into meltdown and ends up seeking medical attention.

"Why do I feel like this?" being answered with "because according to your blood reports you keep eating contraindicated mood meds" is going to fairly quickly lead back home. And, of course, it's really needlessly cruel.

I think I may associate immorality with stupidity. Like any good philosopher king would do, if you believe Plato.

Do I know for sure and am just playing some game? Do I not know and am, but trying to figure it out? Do I not know and am just mental? Hah.

Look at it this way; what I said about people lying to themselves is very valid, because no matter what I say, you cannot trust it and therefore, have to go on your own instinct. You will fill in the blanks.

My side of this conversation is founded on "do not believe a word I say," so you have to decide what you will read into it, and your conclusions are only your own.

What would it look like to speak to a psychopath who was playing games? What would it look like to speak to someone unstable who thinks they're a psychopath and are acting how they believe one would, but is not?

It then isn't a matter of whether you trust me, but of whether you trust yourself. I am not in a position to make that call. Or rather, I am not willing to make that call as it would be 1) potentially mistaken and 2) prone to bias the outcome in unpredictable ways.

Gödel's Incompleteness Theorem of human psychology[16]; at what point in the chain of possible bluffs do you cut loose and just go with your instinct? How justified is anyone in going with their instinct? Eventually we must accept a

---

[16] Gödel's theory is essentially that "Anything you can draw a circle around cannot explain itself without referring to something outside the circle – something you have to assume but cannot prove." It is actually an interesting theory. Gödel created his proof by starting with "The Liar's Paradox" — which is the statement "I am lying."
"I am lying" is self-contradictory, since if it's true, I'm lying, making the statement false; and if it's false, I am lying, so the statement is true. Gödel, in one of the most ingenious moves in the history of math, converted the Liar's Paradox into a mathematical formula. He proved that any statement requires an external observer. Basically, no statement alone can completely prove itself true.

justification as 'base'. But how do we trust ourselves to know when to identify this cutoff? And so it continues.

Dianne
I will have to look for specific areas to answer your question, but in general, it is the same problem that most have by not stopping while you are ahead.

One example is when I mentioned how the fellow used the method of pills to gaslight his victims. Your initial response in the first part of the paragraph was that is deplorable. Okay, anyone would have that reaction. Then you go on to state the reasons why it is deplorable to you being you might get caught.

A non-psychopath would find it deplorable so you would be best left undetected by sticking with that and not expounding on why. Someone who doesn't gaslight wouldn't think about getting in trouble with the authorities but be more focused on it being a deplorable act.

For example, I might say that is deplorable, I hope he gets caught doing such a thing, or I feel sorry for the victims. A scenario of taking things too far and ending up with the authorities involved wouldn't cross my thought process because I don't think in terms of gaslighting.

I hope you understand my example and will wait for your comments before looking for others.

I will give you some more examples later when I return as I will have to read through the emails to develop a couple. In general, it is the thing about starting off with one thought, which can start to sound reasonable then spins off. Along the lines of, I really love my dogs and would never harm them, that is, unless one of them is barking too loud.

Or I never hit women but there was one who really deserved it. That kind of phrasing of things.

I hope you understand that because we don't share visual clues for this conversation of ours, I am only trying to share my reactions. This isn't about judgment it is just about telling my reaction to this particular concept.

What I am trying to say is that if I understand gaslighting correctly, the intent is to cause confusion, anger, anxiety and used to exert control.

I just couldn't see myself thinking that would be a good thing on any level for me. I just don't understand the need to control another person using those techniques. That is why I find the concept and application so interesting because it is such a foreign thing to me.

I can't even think of any reason why I would be motivated to move around keys, keep someone on edge, etc. with gaslighting techniques.

Sure the one about giving drugs is clearly on the far end of the spectrum, but if I am getting it right, it is all about control?

What feelings or benefit comes from seeing another person act like or think they are losing their mind? This is what I am having a difficult time picturing.

I have thought about it for quite a while and really can't think at any time that I would consider doing this to another person.

Fred
I loathe cruelty to animals in any form and will not tolerate violence towards women. I have never raised my hand to a woman, and I suspect that if I ever did it may well result in my killing myself.

The daily cruelty, stupidity and selfishness of large parts of society infuriate and disgust me. Our whole society is built on structures and systems of behavior that are intrinsically harmful and manipulative, coercing those who are worse off into improving the lot of those who are best off.

Sometimes I blame the world for my failings, but other times I do the complete opposite. I want to help people. I want to make the world a better place.

The trouble is, the ways I go about it often end up backfiring badly, which I suppose is the root of my problems; there's something I'm not quite getting right, and I can't tell what it is.

I am not cruel to animals (they are often more tolerable than people, since they don't constantly voice their stupidity), nor am I physically abusive (although I have certainly been involved in fights in the past) and when in my most negative bipolar state can have emotional experiences, albeit in a rather observational manner.

The physical behaviors can manifest (as opposed to being manifested, which is far more normal but entirely different), but in terms of conscious experience I tend to 'feel' a kind of curiosity tinged with contempt at these half-learned reactions.

Additionally, during one of my more excessive bouts of indulgence with narcotics, I had an experience that I believe may have been terror. It was unpleasant enough that I have not revisited it, but it did take me several years to make sense of.

I have never killed or raped. I see violence as an inelegant and crude tool that usually signifies a lack of intelligence.

I am far from unfamiliar with philosophy and there is a saying "justification must stop somewhere." Murder is wrong. Why? Because it causes suffering.

Why is causing suffering wrong? Because... on and on. Sooner or later, you just have to face the brute fact that "murder is wrong" is an expression of value. It doesn't say anything about the world. Nothing. It only says something about the speaker. About their values and commitments and understanding of the world.

I do understand sensibilities, even if I don't share them, so no graphic sexual conquests or reveling in wanton cruelty. At least, not knowingly. Possibly my idea of graphic is far from yours.

Possibly, you consider cruel some things I would consider kindnesses, gifts.

The same applies to action. Why am I doing something? Because, because, because. Sooner or later, "because I want to" is all you've got left. Instead of trying to understand things, observe them. Doodle on them, see what patterns fit. It's all just post-hoc explanations anyway, in the end.

Find what makes sense to you and go with that. An explanation that isn't useful isn't worth coming up with. Therefore, the best explanation is the one most useful to you and your goals.

Dianne
So basically, you don't need to use drugs on your victims because you select people who are easy to control?

Fred
One of the reasons that women – and men, but it is particularly women – get hurt romantically is because of this.

If you have a conception of love so out-there, so Disney-sequel that reality should have intruded on it and replaced it with something remotely realistic by now, you will most likely attract the attentions of someone you will wish you hadn't.

I have a theory that it's because extreme idealizations are something it is very easy to manipulate and very powerful, deeply-rooted motivators.

It allows you to sell an idea to someone who really wants nothing more than to buy it before you even open your mouth. It's buy-before-you-try.

You want this fantasy fulfilled? Well, that's fine. Real melty-eyes and soul-sharing I cannot do. Stories, I can.

That's all emotions are; what would be my ideal life story? Not just "what would it look like?" but also "and how would it feel?" What would the narrative be?

Maybe I am better at this than most because I see my own life as that; a narrative. True? It doesn't really matter. It is made into what it needs to be.

Control the narrative and you control the direction, both of yourself and of anyone else who has bought into the fantasy.

I used to have a lot of fun with one of the music teachers. I didn't take music, but she was the class tutor for my first girlfriend. When things went sour on my first relationship ever, she made the mistake of trying to speak to me, to calm the situation.

Since I was involved in a lot of the school drama productions, I had plenty of opportunities to make her regret this.

She was notoriously easy to make cry anyway, but by the time I left I could make her crumble by just smiling at her a certain way. I had a lot of help on that though, because standard teenage spite contributed a lot to how mental she was already.

She should never have been allowed to teach, really.

Dianne
Can you give me some more examples of gaslighting? We talked about changing the sleep patterns, do you do other things like move keys around (as a small example) that would be considered gaslighting?

Some examples would be great in helping me to understand better.

Additionally, I am curious about what lengths you will go to in order to win. I like the saying of did best rather than did well.

I think that gaslighting seems to take up quite a bit of the relationship to get people to get off balance for better control.

Steve
Gaslighting doesn't take that much time at all really it's just for fun.

I have found that if people don't like who they are, then they let you treat them how you want because they don't think they deserve better treatment.

Fred
I have been thinking. Why does there seem to be such a need to make sense of experiencing such behavior? I can obviously see why it would be unsettling, but why the burning desire to make sense of it? It was what it was. Unfortunate, but no mystery. People seem to find it very hard to accept that.

If it is so repellent, so evil, why risk weaving it into your own tapestry? Gaslighting is often not intentional. At least, not intended to be that. Most of the time, it is a tiny adjustment to a short-term problem.

Example: "I know I said I was going to mow the lawn if it didn't rain on the weekend. I know that you know that. But come on, it's really sunny and there are people I want to go drinking with. I told you I was going to mow the lawn if it didn't rain on the weekend? Doesn't sound likely, since we had a conversation just last week about how it is Blah's birthday this weekend.

"Have you been tricking me into making promises while I'm distracted by other things? Do you ever listen? No babe, that's a rhetorical question.

"You must just be misremembering. I know I did say I'd do it a lot of times last year, so maybe you're remembering one of those times. Well yes, but I only said it so many times because we had such a shitty washout with the weather and the chance never came up.

"Only weekend I remember it not raining last summer was when we were at that wedding. You know the one for your friend where I didn't know anyone and you gave me crap for having a few beers and getting to know people. Or maybe you'd like to do it yourself?

"I don't see you promising to do it any weekend. You're cleaning the rabbits? Fuck the rabbits, they stink and will probably die soon anyway. You wanted them, not me.

"Oh, I'm unreasonable for not just taking on all your chores as well as whatever ones you've created for me already? Fine! Whatever dear, if you're in your insane fantasy palace, then you can ask the Butler to bring me a note. I'll be back later, once you've finished rehashing every past argument and slight you can dredge up from that rap-sheet of yours. "Public Enemy Number One: Fred. Wanted on suspicion of having free will."

Much of that is instinctive, by the way. I 'am' those positions. Sometimes it's a reflex, a way to destabilize people while I find the remote. And all of this here is another ad-hoc explanation.

Maybe I do know what I'm doing, but slip into 'acts' that require I forget it briefly. Maybe I'm really unaware of this behavior at the time.

I know in the past I'd have strongly disagreed with anyone who labeled it 'psychopathic'. Now, it would make a kind of sense. Not that it is all subconscious, of course.

Often – particularly in the past, when I was at more of a loss to explaining the growing gap between how other people describe feeling and how I experience feeling – it isn't conscious. Other times, it most certainly is.

Dianne
Do you mean that sometimes you play games without intending to?

Fred
As I write this, I notice something interesting. Because of the nature of what is at the forefront of my mind, perhaps. There are kind of thought-triggers, entrenched behaviors that I have to be very conscious of.

Am I capable of subconsciously manipulating a position? I can't rule it out.

Other times I catch little things and have to cut them out. I tell you this because I want to highlight how passive a lot of the behavior can be. I can think of times where the 'worse' behavior has been in response to accidentally triggering something with something I hadn't even realized I was doing.

For example, I once reduced a girlfriend to tears of blind rage by doing the fury into calm understanding routine by accident. A quick blow-out was normal and with her usually lasted about 20 minutes. A full strop could last for days and be reliably set off by getting the anger levels up to a decent level and then me suddenly turning into Gandhi.

It's like watching two people agree to jump off something high into water, only for one to suddenly stop at the last minute. It totally throws them. That was not convenient on this occasion, but something (can't even remember what, but I was in the kitchen so it was probably the fridge) distracted me, and I forgot what I was doing.

This meant I replied in a normal, life-is-easy-relaxed voice and 10 minutes later, I was talking to her through the downstairs toilet door while she sobbed on the floor in there.

Initially, she was going on about how could I possibly be so heartless as to apparently not care (as opposed to covertly not caring, which seems to be the accepted norm for human relationships), but she eventually moved on to things she could try to do to stop being such a helplessly dependent, irrational wreck.

You could think of it as being supportive of someone. If you think emotionally, you will be supportive for supportive reasons. If you do not think emotionally, you can be supportive for all sorts of other reasons, too.

It's a tremendously powerful control mechanism because people will actually bully themselves into thinking what otherwise might take a lot of effort to convince them of.

There are learned responses to supportive-type behaviors, which people will lapse into when confronted by them because it is the neurological path of least resistance. They'll feel bad if they don't, because their reward triggers are all set up that way.

They feel unreasonable, irrational, embarrassed, ashamed... none of the things a person who had good reason to be angry would normally feel. So they can't have had good reason to be angry, and the argument was their fault. They're lucky to have someone so patient and supportive, really.

Dianne
You describe it as normal; just as some people write with their left hand, some people gaslight their partners as a regular course of action. Do you have other techniques you can think of?

Fred
I like your comparison to being left-handed. I suppose it is similar; it is an instinctive reaction that then necessitates a particular set of skills and processes to recover from. It could even be the case that half the time it is being done to cover up for the other half the time; why did the car keys move themselves, who promised to do/not do what when, etc.

Oh! I just thought of another possible example: walking out of a room in the middle of a blazing row and quickly getting comfortable and relaxed, only to continue shouting as if I'm still really pissed off.

It's more for the show of things, but if they, then walk in and find me sitting there happily reading a book between adding my yelled responses, I can get a very funny look.

Sounding angry is usually much more useful than actually being angry, because you're more in control and less likely to say something stupid that then needs re-explaining in a way better suited to the intended narrative.

Dianne
You gave me a good example of gaslighting previously around mowing the lawn which I thought was clever. Do you have any other examples that you might share?

Fred
The example of mowing the lawn is fairly every day, as it is about short-term gains and not part of some grand narrative or scheme. To be honest, I may do that far more than I realize. I hope not, but it seems possible.

I've certainly had blazing rows where I've played the victim of cruel and unreasonable expectations or bizarre twists of fate.

As most people want to believe a lie if it keeps their preferred world view intact, often the more outrageous the better. I'd have to be an idiot to think you were stupid enough to believe I am reeking of booze, badly disheveled and have been out all night on some mission of mercy. Obviously, I don't think you're that stupid - as if I would ever!

You know how I feel about stupidity, so why would I be in a relationship with a moron? Ergo I don't think you're that stupid and would never try something so crude and obviously untrue.

Which means it is probably true, because you know I am not that stupid. If I was, I wouldn't win so many arguments.

At no point does this need to be verbalized. The crescent of a love-bite on my shoulder? I was locked out and slept in a hedge, so as not to wake you, which resulted in me waking up with a leech - I know!

In our climate, miles from standing water, too! - On me. I burned the little bastard off though, so hopefully it won't bruise out too badly. I don't think I've used that one before, but it'd be a good blueprint for what is going on: patiently understanding why you may find it hard to believe, showing that we are only even having the discussion because I was putting your needs first.

Then eventually sliding back into the accepted reality of my being great because it is easier and more desirable than confronting the idea that large parts of your life might be a lie. Bits that you'd really rather weren't lies.

Here's a good example of how ingrained some of this stuff can be. I thought, earlier, that if I color coded text and insisted that you include or not include certain colors in this interview, you would go along with it.

Why? Poke, poke, poke, and thar she blows! Not that it would be instructive – not for me, anyway – to do it in this exchange, but I can see great opportunities in a world where coloring text was usual. Lots of different shades, alternating for no obvious reason. Not obviously no reason, though. That's boring. Something to be read into, guessed at.

It doesn't matter if something actually is clever, half the time. Only the nagging curiosity as to why I'm doing it. It's like going around a house very slightly tilting all the paintings. Zero damage. Tiniest of adjustments.

They don't even need to matter to other people, but for some reason, people always choose that they must. Is your world really so fragile that it requires right angles? Yet you find Pandora's Box and don't just open in but stuff yourself in there for a closer look.

Reality = scared of acute angles. Ideal = intrepid explorer of worlds unknown. Which do you expect to be shown? What is going to get me what I want? You are getting what you want. The phrase "buyer's remorse" springs to mind.

Some thoughts on gaslighting:
I like this term. This is actually really quite straight forward, at least as I view it:
    1) You started it.
    2) You request it.

Dianne
Does this mean you think it is the victim's fault if they are being controlled by your gaslighting them?

Fred
By (1), I mean imagine what it is like to live in a world where people do things that make no sense. They act against all reason. They suddenly change their mind, usually to something even more stupid than whatever it already was. They give gibberish explanations, superficial descriptions that sound more meaningful than they really are.

There is an invisible game being played and failing to play it can make people really, really angry. And you can't just do the moves. You have to think special thoughts as well, while you're doing them. As if doing something isn't what feeling something means anyway.

I am blamed for my perceived failures at playing this invisible, pieceless game on some occasions. Yet, in the same breath; I am criticized for my exceptional technical talents on others. So tell me, am I too good or not good enough? Dracula or Frankenstein?

Both, I note, also creations of others. Anyway, my point with (1) is this: I grew up in a society that was gaslighting me from day zero. It is normal behavior. I am just better at it, because I don't get lost in my own fantasy along the way.

Or maybe I just get lost in mine more successfully, if that is what it is.

By (2), I mean 'asked for it' in the literal sense. It's a tool of instruction, teaching you to trust me more than yourself. You want to trust me more than yourself, because I make better decisions than you do.

Why do the weak look to the strong? For protection. Without ever stopping to wonder how the strong got that way. We don't photosynthesize, you know.

There's the perception that if you give a strong person a helping hand to the top, they'll reward you later. This is absurd. If they were in the business of carving up and dishing out their strength, they wouldn't be strong.

If you are weak and you want to find contentment, peace... do not look to someone strong. If you think, you need a strong partner, you probably only want a strong partner. Why? Because you wish you were stronger yourself.

I had an ex that said several times "I need someone strong, so I can stop and be weak sometimes." Sometimes?

She barely even counted as a vertebrate. Not only are you chasing a want rather than a need, but it is a want that by definition you should not be chasing. Sheep don't play with wolves for a reason.

No matter how much fun all the rough play may look. It isn't play. Not for you, anyway. If you wish, you were stronger, be stronger. That is the only answer. Decide what you want to be and be it. The only answer to anything, I mean.

Do not invite a strong person into your life in place of choosing to be strong yourself. Be strong yourself and you shall soon see how the invitations start rolling in.

Dianne
You said earlier that you controlled people by gaining their trust. Doesn't that require some degree of being understanding rather than being hypercritical?

Fred
Of course, I sound understanding; I know what cues an understanding person would give. Of course, I am easy to talk to, because people trust those who share their views and conclusions and therefore, drop their guard in ways they would not to someone who was more critical.

Of course, I seem nonjudgmental; I do not share your judgment metric. However, most of all, of course, I listen.

That is how to learn, after all; your password, your alarm code, where you keep your valuables. Which buttons do what? Is this really not just what everyone does? Honestly? I cannot believe people do not. Don't you?

Dianne
Do your victims eventually recognize what you are doing when you use gaslighting as a part of your agenda to control them?

Fred
I think it is possible there is an element of some people seeing gaslighting where there is none.

Once the paranoia sets in, every little disagreement, each time you can't find something, or you suffer bad luck, there is going to be a growing temptation to see it as something more.

On the one hand, I can see how it would be difficult for a normal person to cope with that kind of environment for long. On the other, I think perhaps... none of you have any idea how lucky you are.

The glimmer of part of the dream being realized, and you run in panic. I didn't have anyone to explain this to me. I had to work it out for myself. You can have a guide. An instructor. It's shaking you out of your delusions about what 'really' matters, about what your words and thoughts really mean.

That said you will see the reality rather than the ideal. Increasingly. And caricatures of both, some empowering and others petrifying. In the traditional sense, in that they will turn parts of the world to stone for you. Parts of you.

I've heard that, before. "What you said turned my stomach to stone". That's a lesson. That sensation – the one with the look of incomprehension, tears welling and looking like you're trying to crawl out of our own throat. Is that how it feels; like crawling out of your own throat? It is how it looks.

But it's a lesson in how the world really works. It is saying, "Don't worry. See, I am a dab hand at this! You're safe with me." I think, maybe; it is when a desire to show off falls outside accepted behavioral norms. Why don't you love me more for this? I remember thinking that a few years ago.

It was like a light bulb went out in her eyes, and she had no idea where or who she was. I have just shown you; look how good I am. Look how much you can learn. Look how safe you are. Look how easy it could all be. Yet NO approval? None? No credit?

And you want to be a strong person, yet the first time I show you – teach you, give you – strength you act like I just stabbed a bunny at Easter.

As I said, people don't know what they need. They never think what would be required to prop up their dream, just so long as they get it. Bacon may get many people drooling, but they've no stomach for slaughtering the pig to get at it.

They just want bacon. Not murder and mess and confronting the full unflattering reality of their self-interest. Compartmentalize. What outcome do I want? Forget the means, just give me the ends.

But I think in reality, it is a futile gesture. People oppress themselves. You could probably no more exist in the moment, revel in the chaos than I could... there's the rub. I don't know, because I can't.

After this although, what happens? You see something you don't like and what do you do, nearly always? Come crawling back, begging to say it was all a trick, that you imagined it; you misheard, misunderstood... anything, but that it was true.

Always. More. Lies. Just one last hit, just this time, just so everything can be okay again. But it never ends and sooner, or later, you overdose. Over the edge of comfortable existence and into the land of uncomfortable truth.

That petrified thing can't be ignored anymore and half the time you're wandering around like you've got shell shock or some kind of hyper-mundane PTSD. Waiting, stunned and vacant, floating about until you drift back to terra firma again.

Over and over and over again, never willing to take a jump but destined to take the fall. People gaslight themselves.

Dianne
You are again acting like you are the victim here and blaming the victims for being gaslighted. What would you say to the victims who post on my forum?

Fred
I do not mean to paint myself as a victim. The point to take away from it is this: if victims want to stop being tossed about in all this, they need to stop thinking like victims.

Stop trying to understand. Stop trying to empathize. Most of all, stop trying to fight the lesson being taught; the world is not as safe, nice, or fluffy as you want it to be, and unless you face this fact then you're going to be basically helpless forever.

If people really find the lesson even a fraction as traumatic as they make it out to be, I would have thought it all the more valuable that they actually bother to learn it.

I think the rule should be something like this: if you are doing something 'every day' and routine, you should not expect to be at risk just by existing in that part of life.

If you are doing something that you know makes you vulnerable (romantic relationship, business deals, underground street fights) or something that should raise your suspicions (offer that sounds too good to be true, in whatever context), then you carry some responsibility for looking out for yourself.

It doesn't excuse the person who exploits you, but you can't complain too loudly either. Being naive is no defense against culpability in the same way that being ignorant is no defense against breaking the law.

Dianne
Do you use gaslighting frequently outside of your close relationships?

Fred
Gaslighting is a tough one. As mentioned, I think my own particular traits only emerge most severely in intimate relationships.

Also, it isn't so much that it's a key element of relationships as an inevitable consequence of things starting to fall apart. Hah! I've just realized; if I am mirroring, perhaps all gaslighting really comes down to is the fact I'm mirroring their own confusion and uncertainty right back at them in the way I deal with things.

Certain in your love for me? No problem, I will respond accordingly. Not so sure? That's probably going to end in tears. I don't set out to do it, so it isn't a case of thinking "oh, she is doing my head in this week, so I'm going to constantly move her house keys around every time she puts them down." It's more of a reactive process, like on-the-fly problem solving.

Patching the reality back together to keep the dream alive. In terms of pre-mediated actions, the two big ones are completely barefaced lying without remorse and deciding someone needs to decide to leave me. Those I'm afraid I must admit I do consciously do and will put a lot of effort and patience into, if I feel it is required.

Dianne
Isn't that passive-aggressive behavior by you, behaving in a negative way so that someone will leave you instead of you breaking up with them?

Fred
I think sometimes it may come from a misplaced sense of fun, actually. Instead of taking the situation as seriously as would be expected, a kind of 'disrespectful' refusal to get worked up over things that don't really matter can take hold.

This might be out of place jokes in the middle of arguments, or it could be something very minor and childish, like a tiny pseudo-prank.

For example, I had a falling out with some manipulative beast of a girl some years ago but still had reason to have to visit the house she lived in. I'm not sure why, but if the toilet paper were the 'wrong way' on the toilet roll holder she would become incredibly irate.

You can probably work out what I started doing. That was all I did and the whole time I saw it as a kind of joke, like I was saying by my actions "look, we are both sharing in the joke that we know the idea of being upset by this is absurd." But playfully "don't even think of trying to mess with me, because I've already got you figured out," too.

As it turned out on this occasion, she was trying to get her claws into a friend of mine, and eventually her plans blew up in her face with barely any encouragement from me at all. Frankly, I could probably have stayed out of it completely, and it'd have ended just the same. Things tend to, sadly.

There's also the teaching element, trying to show people when they're clinging to an absurd or damaging belief. Self-limitation.

The lessons are rarely if ever direct though, as that's part of the point; stop thinking about things the same old ways, pay attention, and you might find greater understanding and insight into things. External and internal. See the other patterns that you're usually blind to, leave your bias at the door.

As I said to you before; think poetically. If you only ever try to understand things one way, you will only ever get one set of conclusions regarding them, and you'll never really have the slightest idea how they work or what they mean.

But it has to be earned; the puzzles have to be worked through; you have to practice to get good at the game... otherwise they are worthless because the lessons mean nothing to you, they have no value, and you have exchanged no effort for another item of information that you don't really understand or appreciate.

Nothing says, "Get some perspective, and you'll be happier for it" more clearly than breaking down into tears because the loo roll is facing one direction rather than the other.

The first step to recovery is admitting you have a problem. Namely, that reality is a carefully constructed lie to make us feel safe. Stop trying to feel safe and start trying to tactually learn things.

This means you have to learn to let go of the tiny meaningless details like lavatorial Feng Shui. It also means you have to learn to stop worrying about the ground and enjoy the view and the rush of the fall. That bit isn't so easy and probably doesn't suit everyone.

I mean... does it matter?! It's as absurd as thinking a supremely powerful being would care what days you go to work, how many penises there are in a single relationship or about winning your adulation enough to manifest its image on a piece of toast. None of these things are important, but people will quite literally start wars over them.

They will kill each other before stopping and honestly examining their beliefs.

When they successfully avoid looking honestly at themselves, they can often feel overwhelmed with orgasmic joy as a reward. Like the stick and carrot of mental slavery. They are the immoral and the mentally ill, the ones who bring misery and suffering and hate to the world in such vast quantities.

They are the ones who will destroy the world rather than admit that their delusions are just that and there is nothing remarkable, interesting or significant about them in any way.

Perhaps extreme stupidity or insecurity should start being treated as a mental illness or personality disorder in itself, because to be honest I absolutely refuse to believe that most people are as stupid and ignorant as they appear to be. Or rather, I refuse to believe that they are stupid and ignorant to such an extent for any reason other than intellectual laziness and cowardice.

Dianne
Do you have a difficult time sustaining a relationship? Does the "mirroring" you mentioned earlier help you to relate to others?

Fred
I do have a very strong survival instinct and evidently some fairly major and damaging baggage when it comes to certain interpersonal contexts. This means that when I feel cornered and

threatened I react in ways that may be considered gaslighting or designed to undermine self-confidence. It also means I'm more likely to feel like that in a romantic relationship because of the other issues.

On the mirroring point, think of it like this: people do things that would suggest they want X or Y all the time, even though if you asked them, they would say they do not want that thing.

There is also disconnection between want and need. Too full of your own magnanimity but in reality, incapable of compromise? Maybe a reminder that your senses and memory are not perfect and therefore, not the basis for laying down the law would be what you need, even though you're very unlikely to want it.

The other point is that mirroring isn't always about desire, but about current behavior. If you act aggressively, you are more likely to be met with a greater degree of aggression than if you'd initially acted in a more conciliatory fashion.

If you act kindly, people are more likely to respond with kindness of their own. There are established patterns (moves in our interpersonal games) that everyone depends on being able to understand and exploit.

Some are just very bad at it and keep making all the wrong moves (here I have in mind people who are violently aggressive as the worst 'players', but it could also be the moist-palmed apologists who would fold in a light breeze, so loudly do they broadcast their lack of a spine). Anyway, this is something ALL people do, to some extent, and the standard for most is actually fairly significant.

With my particular set of psychological building blocks, I am perhaps more prone to reflecting people's uncertainty, confusion, bitterness, anger, etc. than most.

Dianne
Isn't this just another way to exercise control over the other person?

Fred
Personally, speaking, confusion and anger both seem plausible goals. Anxiety can be an unfortunate side-effect of this, but isn't exactly desirable. I suppose technically you could say it is setting out for control, but I'd argue that's the only reason anyone ever does anything; to influence their environment in some way. That's what doing something is.

I'm sure there are those out there who want to control the other person for the sake of control, but I am not one of them. I would say... I do it to guide people or as a kind of knee-jerk reaction when I feel threatened in some way.

If it is premeditated, then it is not maliciously so, but if it's reactive, then 'lashing out' would be a fair term.

With a couple of very particular exceptions, I suppose. I would take great pleasure in watching a couple of people crumble into half-sane ruin, and if I was given the opportunity, I'm not sure I'd be able to resist getting a few kicks in to help them on their way down. But then nobody is perfect, so I imagine I'm by no means unusual in this regard.

Dianne
You say you do this to guide people or to react to a threat, but you also say you enjoy destroying people. Do you think this is normal?

Fred
The general sense of it is that I don't gaslight in the ways your rather more psychotic friend [Steve] with the meds does, nor do I do it simply for pleasure or entertainment. It would be a poor sport, even if I did have the inclination, anyway.

Making a crazy person crazy? Some great achievement that would be.

Like shooting up an intensive care unit and claiming it as a famous victory. I should have gone with "fish in a barrel," shouldn't I?

I do it out of self-preservation or a desire to help. I realize I might be stretching the accepted methodology beyond that used by, say, motivational speakers or behavioral therapists.

I also believe I get much, much better results in most cases. Those types of people (speakers and therapists) work from the top down. I work from the bottom up. Don't treat the symptoms, treat the cause.

I wonder if I'm subconsciously going around creating coping strategies for other people in the same way as I create them for myself. "Oh, you don't know how to stand up for yourself. Everyone does when they're pushed hard enough though, so let's do that" or "You're altogether too full of your own worth.

Let's show you what reality behind the curtain is like, teach some humility." But many more subtle, nuanced and particular things than this too. To wake someone from a deep sleep, sometimes it is necessary to give them a sudden shock.

Gaslighting is a wonderful tool for doing this because it teaches them the first and most important lesson; your beliefs are not unshakeable and your perspective is not infallible, so learn to stop and examine them very closely and without a trace of sentimentality.

To get them to see the duck, you may have to startle them into forgetting about the rabbit for a time. The hope is to be able to then switch between both at will.

Dianne
Are you really expecting me to believe that you manipulate people for their own good, rather than for your desire to control them?

Fred
I think I'm very nearly able to do that. Since I'm apparently better at it than a lot of people, this can quickly spiral out of control and people get much, much more upset than I ever intended.

I can only hold my hands up and say that, looking at the evidence of my own actions from this perspective, I apparently don't care about not hurting them as much as I care about not losing. Note not "not losing them," although I may feel this is the motivation at the time.

There are, however, these occasions when someone has become so dangerous/unreasonable that a more emphatic lesson needs to be learned. If someone has no concept of consequences and think they can throw hysterical, spoilt tantrums to get their own way, I shall be sure to remind them that crocodile tears will be rewarded by my turning them into real tears. In great amounts.

In fact, I'd go as far as to say that I only cross into overtly controlling when I feel someone is trying to do the same to me. That makes me a bit crazy, if I'm honest. It is the most reliable way to get me up to DEFCON 1[17] in no time at all and the response is usually a rather uncompromising demonstration of "do not think you can control me."

And what better way to show someone how little control they have over you by showing them that they can't even stop you from controlling them?

What more neatly and ironically delicious way to teach such an important lesson? Again, it's mirroring - if you treat me with disrespect, then I will do the same in return.

---

[17] The defense readiness condition (DEFCON) is an alert state used by the United States Armed Forces. DEFCON 5 is normal peacetime readiness; DEFCON 1 is maximum force readiness.

If you ignore all the warnings, convince yourself you're more intelligent, in possession of more insight into people than I am and try to take advantage of me, when it all blows up in your face, and you have to face your own insecurities, it really is your fault.

Try to control me and I will not only control you, but my survival instinct dictates that I must also neutralize the threat of you ever trying to do it again. The worst cases, the ones where I can't really excuse my actions on any other grounds, are when this happens.

The closest I will ever let someone get to win in these situations is Mutually Assured Destruction. Thoroughly dismantling their psyche and then beating the remains into submission is preferred and, so far, the worst result I've had.

When there's nothing worth saving, disarm the threat, prevent it recurring and leave whatever is left to live out its life in peace.

Dianne
Is it possible that few, in fact, know they are getting the gaslighting treatment? In order for it to be effective, I would think it would take pretty good skills and part of the equation would be to do it and not have them detect it?

Have many or any of your partners, in reality, caught on and commented as such; I am also guessing that if they did the

game would shift to a higher level to not be so exposed.

I guess what I am suggesting is the reason that in all these year's very few victims at my forum have actually said much about gaslighting is because they weren't aware that it was really what was driving them down the rabbit hole?

Fred
I meant more retrospectively, once they are out of the situation. I've never been picked up on doing it. Since most of the time, I don't realize until afterwards myself, I can only assume the same goes for others as, they by definition have less idea what is going on than I do.

I honestly don't know how I'd react if confronted. Not that I'd ever expect to be, since most people are happy in their blinkered ignorance.

Typing that, my mind landed on two tangents; "accuse them of projection" and "very sarcastic admission." I hope that is helpful as I don't relish these moments of staring right at my own faults.

I really did not want to use the word faults. I have been having some very interesting thoughts recently, and one of them is that I intensely dislike the idea this could be controlling me far more than it ever controls other people. If so, that is wholly unacceptable.

Dianne
When you say "retrospective," that is consistent with the comments by members at my forum.

The victims rarely mention gaslighting as the cause of their distress, although it seems evident to me that it is a key element in the relationship. When they do mention it, it is from a "rear-view mirror" perspective.

Fred
It is important to remember that my perspective will be only mine, so I can't comment on how significant it may be for others. For me, it is nearly always reactive, and it's possible I do it more than I think.

For others, such as Mr. Mood Meds [Steve], it's obviously something they take more seriously, but... hmmm. How to put this? This depends on whether my understanding of things is correct, but I'll try to explain it.

Maybe it is more common than I think, and others revel in it. My appreciation of playing a game well without resorting to cheating may mean my view is skewed. Much of this is "in the rear-view mirror" for me too, in many ways, as I'm trying to make sense of myself, my behaviors, what drives me and what I am and am not.

Others who are more self-aware or just have a crueler set of tastes may well be very different from me.

But from my perspective, I would say it is more about retaining control. By the time it starts, I am responding to losing control over the disintegration of the fairytale that was the relationship up until then. In a few cases - the fake conversations or the punishment of someone really vile - it goes beyond this, but for the most part, it's part of the set, the backdrop to the main performance.

It also seems plausible that I feel the need to compete on some other level than is obvious; to you or to myself, perhaps.

I also want to reiterate that I do not think in terms of gaslighting, either. That's the whole point; it is something that I only usually recognize retrospectively, as at the time it is instinctive problem-solving that only later adds up to such behavior.

I realize that I may have sounded misleading in the way I've been considering things, but it is important to bear in mind how detached and analytic I am being when discussing them. Those aren't conscious thoughts and reasoning, but explanations that identify behavior as what may be taken by others to be such-and-such.

That and speculation on the role they play in any systematized behavior that can be traced through an individual's ongoing life patterns; dysfunctional relationships, impulsive behavior, mercurial nature, social mirroring, extreme over-analysis and so forth.

CHAPTER FIVE
Relationships

"Trust that man in nothing who has not a conscience in everything."
— Laurence Sterne

Dianne
We've discussed how you think about yourself. Are there some things that partners tell you that stand out? For example, do either you or they claim to be soul mates?

Do you have exclusive relationships or are there others on the side, so to speak? Do they ever find out about each other if this is the case?

Fred
What my girlfriend would think? Not a lot, I would imagine. No idea. She'd probably write all sorts of nasty stuff under the guise of having tried to understand and help me. She was an eternal victim no matter what happened.

After a while, the inclination is to assume that's because she wants to be and to meet that need in her. I do not know what she would write, nor do I care.

She was a terminally broken mess, and frankly; I think she enjoys the attention too much to ever stop.

Steve
All of my ex-partners have said that I was emotionally disconnected, and they don't seem to feel wanted by me in a loving way. I have always been faithful, but I play mind games with them to put doubt in their heads.

Dianne
How far into the relationships did they say they found you emotionally disconnected? If, for example, you are in a relationship for a couple of years how long into the relationship do they typically start making this comment?

Do you wonder why they stay if they find this to be the case? Is there some feeling that they are trying to fix you and think they can make a better connection? Are there some examples of how they might try to fix the situation?

Steve
It is normally about one year into my relationships that people say I'm emotionally disconnected, but it is something they think is fixable or their fault. I normally try to find girls that have low self-esteem, or I use that year to lower it a bit or play the damaged card, so they feel I need saving in which case they try to be more loving to get me to change.

But they never think that I was never connected, but I just made them think I was to get them to fall for me. I also hear a lot, "You need to open up to me."

I never quite get that? I mean I thought I was open because I tell them what I want so I get it. However, they mean emotionally and I'm not emotional, so I'm stuck making up things to seem walled off in an emotional sense.

It's just annoying because then if stories conflict, then it just goes on and on from there.

It takes about one year to call me emotionally disconnected because there is a bit of breathing room at the start with getting to know each other (three-four months) then month six to seven they are so in love that they forgive me for not connecting yet, until month ten I get away with pretending that

I connected because I start to tell them I love them, but that tends not to last so it works out to be a year. Then they tend to try to fix me over the next year.

When I am told I need to open up more I have told them my life goals and ambitions. It's not like I keep them secret really anyway. I just leave out the part about them not being there when I get what I want.

Dianne
It is interesting to me that it takes people/partners a year to start thinking that you are emotionally disconnected. Do you know why that is, because a year seems like a long time for someone to tune into that?

Could it be that you don't see them often, or that they spend most of this year focused on telling you about themselves?

Steve
When I meet a girl, I do all I can to make them think that we were made for each other.

It is easy because I can read what they want, and they all say I'm a good listener which is kind of funny because they're telling me all I need to manipulate them or to make them think that we have a lot in common, or I feel the same way.

Fred
I can be a superb listener, people often remark that they're surprised how easy they find me to talk to, how nonjudgmental I am. At the same time, I can often give insights into people's behaviors that they would not, because their view is twisted by the 'gravity' of their emotional reasoning.

Very rarely does someone ask, "What should I do?" wanting to hear anything other than "exactly what you want to do." I find it almost impossible to believe that most people aren't aware of this in themselves.

People trust the well-spoken, tall, dark stranger with the blazing eyes because on some level, they have been married to him since they were young, in some fantasy.

It's like being handed a script. A shopping list. Buy me these things and I will do your bidding. It is being asked to do it!

Be careful what you wish for, because no sane person turns down the offer of power and reward, freely offered, let alone begged to accept.

People use me to try to make themselves 'whole'. This usually lasts up to the stage where they feel they really want to know the 'real' me, who often by this point has been pumped up to such mythological fascinating levels that it becomes a life goal for them to find out.

I've understood them like no-one else ever has, after all! So quickly, so effortlessly!

It is no wonder they're often the same types interested in other types of con; they want magical solutions and are easy to cold-read. For me, it's me. The idea of me. Their idea of me.

I have lost count of the number of times I have heard "I had given up on ever finding 'the one'." I tend to laugh and tell them that was wise. That always gets a good response, for some reason.

Who is manipulating who, here? I just told the truth. But think about it... why would anyone ever say that? It is clearly a disarming remark, but in a context where disarming remarks are supposedly not needed.

Nobody tells someone they distrust that they think they're "the one," the embodiment of their hopes and dreams, so what is it doing in the conversation? Maybe you can add that to your red flag's list, if you like; apparently charming/witty, trust-winning behavior that is out of place.

Although good luck noticing them at the time.

Dianne
The question comes to mind, are there places where you find it best to meet partners? How do you find partners with low self-esteem?

For example, some people like meeting them online, others perhaps bars, etc. Even though you may not completely isolate them from their family do you spend time with them and their family?

Do you ever let them meet your family?

Steve
I have always found it easy to read people and what they want and always thought of what those people are useful for.

Low self-esteem is something that is easy to pick up when you are looking for it. In today's world, you might as well look for people with decent self-esteem because it's quicker in the way that there's less and less each day.

However, for me fidgeting and mumbling and posture along with, eye contact or eye direction (looking down and not at things when stopped)

Meeting people, um, well, it's more places like McDonald's and supermarkets that I go for because you can pick up more about them from the food they eat and the way they act. I have found that watching people when they don't think they're being watched gives you a good idea of their mindset.

I spend time with the families as do they, but I have to act a lot around them to keep them out of the way, but they tend to like the way I want their daughter to get her life together.

I make my partners get more skilled in the way of their choice as a consolation prize for the fact that we have no future with each other; I pay for it and all.

Fred

In terms of meeting new partners, that's a tough one. I sometimes go a year or so without any, just doing my own thing. When one then turns up, it could be anything from an old friend (oddly common; however weird it may be; I seem to become the object of slowly developing attractions that can then turn into obsessions.

I don't intentionally start these, but they seem to happen, and I've been out with far more friends than can be healthy) to someone I just met at a bar. Online is good, but I don't know whether that's just because I'm articulate in writing and probably more confident in talking to the person and not their own social façade.

Which maybe links into the isolation point, thinking about it; I tend to find I like people more when they're being more themselves than when they're being whatever they think they should be in a social situation. Everyone does it, all the time, without even thinking.

I have a liking for people who are determinedly themselves and don't bow to social pressures or convention, but also a soft spot for those 'downtrodden' types who wish they could be more themselves. Maybe I see the former as kindred spirits and the latter as prospective students, I don't know.

The subconscious is one hell of a playground to lose things in.

I do not prowl. I do not hunt. I simply seek out companionship and follow my heart, often all too easily. All the other stuff - whatever it may be - comes later. Nobody ever really gets hurt unless they get too close, I suppose.

Either that or I've misjudged 'really getting hurt' and am oblivious to a whole extra layer of destruction, which is a magnificently depressing thought.

I would very much like the world to not be better off without my having existed.

In terms of isolation, I guess I don't see it in that way. It is two people getting to know each other as completely as possible. That is best done in isolation, and it doesn't need to be engineered as it is desired by both parties.

When it comes to how to find these people, that's pretty much irrelevant because they sure as hell know how to find me. Moths to a flame.

As I said, people develop strange fascinations with me, often when they initially may write me off as not of interest to them. Over time, I think my various comments, looks and ideas end up suggesting that I'm not, say, a brash drunk with little interest in deeper questions. Or my off-kilter views gradually get interpreted as wisdom and people want to know more and where it comes from. Arrogant? Hugely! But I think true, too.

What is the 'pay off', as you would say? Being the center of someone's universe. Being something so wonderful that you bring them unaccustomed joy and hope. Changing the way they see themselves. I think it's a validation thing, because I can't really give it for myself and the more fanatical, it is the clearer their adoration.

Maybe if I'm missing out on minutiae, then grand gestures/expressions are the only way for me to be sure I'm reading a person's sincerity and emotional state correctly? Speculative, but it'd fit.

I've often said to a couple of my closest friends that I'd make a good cult leader, and it could be a future career. Jokingly, of course. One of them responded to the suggestion I go into politics with "that's the most dangerous idea I've ever heard; he'd be running the world in a week and no-one would know how or why."

Dianne
I spent some time researching cult leaders, and they are all psychopaths. I found an interesting one who was part of a religious/eastern religious group close to where I lived so I could observe them at a

closer range. It is interesting to me how people are drawn in.

People don't feel heard so I would think it would be quite easy to get them to tell you all their weaknesses and not be really realizing what they are doing. Just like a good therapist wouldn't have any clients if people had friends who actually listened to them.

Fred
On the relationship-finding front, I suppose I'm attracted to people who are vulnerable, and I perceive myself as being able to help a lot. I've always thought of this as selfish, good and normal for any morally aware person. Now I'm wondering whether it's because I'm being drawn for other reasons and have just rationalized it as that.

I spend a lot of time down that particular rabbit hole, second/third/Nth guessing my own motives, just as much as I do those of others. Dispassionately and objectively, for the most part, mine or other people.

Whatever the reason, I can see very easily when someone has the invisible scars that life's worst events leave on the mind. What I find strangest of all is I rarely if ever have to broach whatever topic it is; people seem eager to tell me, to unburden themselves. And that is fine. After all, what else am I doing here?

Dianne
There is something attractive about a good listener; women tend to swoon if someone really listens to them, probably more so than a man's reaction.

I see it more as the data-collecting phase. That's when you bring yourself into play by starting to speak about being portrayed as the victim. Keep in mind that naturally these are just my observations.

Playing the role of the victim or whatever is the term will actually bring out the mothering to "let me fix this guy." Also wouldn't playing the victim set the stage if the conquest finds out something terrible about your past? It would beat them to the punch with how horrible it was for you for this to happen.

Essentially, you could take no responsibility but bring out the protective side of the person in the net, right?

Fred
I suppose I play the victim in the persona of a misunderstood outcast. People want to bring me into the fold. They want to understand me, to help me understand myself, so I can find 'peace'.

That's what makes me so attractive to certain kinds of people; they're burbling empaths who are on some road to recovery themselves and can't bear to see someone left behind alone, suffering.

Still in the denial phase, where I'm telling myself, it's all okay.

Where they were in the past, where they think they're getting away from. And what better way to show to themselves their new strength than by offering it without question? This is not premeditated, but an appraisal of why I think I've adopted certain guises over others.

They work better or with less upkeep or some other advantage that suits my particular tendencies. And women love mystery. I'm full of that. Or rather, devoid of answers, which I suppose must look the same from a distance.

They love a rogue. Bad boy is all well and good, but it attracts attention and most women learn that one fairly early simply because most men are bastards. They can't help it any more than I can help being me, or you can help being you.

Dianne
The victim concept is an interesting one to me, and I appreciate reading your thoughts. I do have to agree with you and when someone is handed a map to the treasure how can we then blame them when we fall "victim" to the charms.

Fred
Attraction-signaling behavior is extremely hard to ignore. It would be like walking past free money or poisoning my own food. I could do it, but it seems unlikely in the extreme that I will ever choose to.

The idea of pursuit is misunderstood. I have never really gone in for seeking people out. There is almost never a need, as the right kind of people tends to seek me out.

It is even better this way, because I know I have attracted them effortlessly or even in light of some artificial obstacle I wanted to test myself against.

So yes, there is certainly a viewpoint that victims create themselves. Or are not victims at all, but addicts who are unwilling to address their weakness for their drug of choice. Friends have remarked that I 'collect crazies' which I find highly amusing. Yes, I do! What a masochist I am! When will I ever learn, eh? It. Is. All. So. Obvious.

I have attracted many girls who have had highly emotional temperaments. Partly, because the stronger and more frequent the feedback the better, I admit. But also to learn. Without learning, how can we function in a society that is so neurotic and emotionally-obsessive?

Dianne
Are we all in need of finding someone to fill some void that we can't find within ourselves? Are we uncomfortable with the concept of being okay with being alone, and it doesn't have to spell being lonely? In any situation, it really does take both parties to participate.

These are areas that I hope we can explore in more depth because I have always been interested in this conversation, but frankly, it would be a difficult one to approach at my forum. I am afraid it would make the members feel I didn't empathize with their plight, but I very much do.

I agree about the addictive behavior and also think it stems from simply not having clear boundaries. The lacking of clear boundaries keeps people searching for the answers outside of themselves and living a life painting those red flags white.

Fred
I sometimes overstep boundaries. Maybe I allow other people to spiral out of control and assume they've got a tab on things and are just having a bit of fun feeling alive. I don't run someone over in the street because I didn't know I wasn't supposed to. I can see why that is 'bad'.

People make such an abominable fuss over things as stupid as being interested in the one of an endless stream of babies.

They don't like that I show them their own lack of control, their own hypocritical delusions by not conforming to them. Subverting them. Making them better and getting more from them than they do.

Having read a little more on the matter today – other accounts, support, advice and so forth – I really appreciate the irony of how the ways to 'recover from' a sociopath read like a check-list of how to become more like one. Have you ever noticed this?

I'm only trying my best to fit in, like everyone else. There have been occasional comments though, from friends or people I've only just met or girlfriends, along the lines that my reasoning "is right in all the wrong ways."

There are also a few people who know me really well (relatively, of course) who would describe me something like "a nice guy who you really don't want to piss off. Then he gets crazy." Hah! I remembered a recent one.

My house mate asked how something or other went, and I said what I thought and why. He smiled and said, "you never play one game when you can play five, do you?" Is this the sort of thing you want?

Dianne
Don't they catch on after a while? How long do your relationships last? Were you the one who ended the relationships or was it them? Is it a clean break or do you continue to see them from time to time?

Steve
All but one ex I have made break up with me. That one didn't seem to get the hints and stayed too long. I normally like a partner for two to four years, and the longest was six years but that seems to have been too long because she has gone mad from it and has been committed three times, so I think I will stick to a four-year maximum.

All of my ex's still talk to me and think I'm a nice guy even after what I put them through. I tend to make them think it's their fault for everything.

Fred
I have been told by several people – mostly vulnerable women – that they find me slightly unsettling because I see right through them. The fact that they have gone on to tell me that should tell you that this wasn't enough to stop them going on to open up to me, often with a truly eyebrow-raising level of trust.

Because I trapped them? Tricked them? No. Because they wanted to.

To be clear, there are many people whose trust I have never abused, as there has never been any purpose in doing so or even hold a kind of fondness for them.

There are whole sequences of my life, which would be identical in form to those of a genuinely supportive, kind person. I won't even bother to pretend that I've not exploited or mistreated anyone, particularly if they've given me reason to view them with contempt.

It is not my fault if people want to believe idiotic things. I never get the acclaim for how happy they are while the lie – their lie, I might emphasize - lasts, so why should I unquestioningly take responsibility for the bit afterwards where they don't want it to end? They're not mad at me. Well, they are, but they shouldn't be.

What they're really angry about is having been made a fool of so easily.

From my perspective, I would say that I just do not quit when the going gets tough and will do whatever I can to save a relationship. If it is, then obviously not one that can be saved, I will give the other person the power to be the one who leaves. Aren't these good qualities? That's an honest question.

Although I will admit that the them leaving thing has other various benefits that would probably make it worth doing anyway.

Maybe I just mean "I want to make you happy" differently to how others mean it. More literally; I will make you happy. More intelligent, less scared, more stable, better equipped and more self-aware than you would be otherwise, because I'm helping you strip out all the crap and dead wood that's holding you back.

I think, reading that back, I shall stop short of claiming to teach modesty.

Bill

If anyone has seen behind my "mask," they have yet to be brave enough to say anything. Most of what I've heard directly has been, as I said earlier, that I can be intimidating.

I have heard indirect reports that I scare some people, particularly when they are opposing me on something. When this has been brought to my attention, there are very little specifics.

They can't describe what exactly they are scared of or what they think they will do. So the reports have never went very far or taken very seriously by superiors.

Dianne
Do you find that you need to wear a "mask" to relate to others? Is this just another word for lying? On the forum, I've seen it said that people know a psychopath is lying because his lips are moving.

Bill
When I speak of the average person wearing a mask, I do not mean that they have intent to deceive. On the contrary, when they are masked it is often with the best intentions.

When you listen to someone's god-awful boring story about their children's first day at school and feign interest, is that not a mask? When you know what someone is saying is absolutely absurd, but you fight the urge to say so, is that not a mask?

The difference between us is you do it because of social contract that requires politeness. I do it, so they can believe I am truly interested in them. We all wear masks; I just make my masks profitable. Notice, I use the plural; masks. I wear many.

Fred
You reference the ever-present phrase "you know they're lying because their lips are moving." From my point of view, I am lying no more than you. Less, perhaps. I tell the same kinds of lies, but I don't believe them myself.

That is the difference. Or maybe it isn't – I apparently do not and possibly cannot know. When I speak, you lie. When you speak, you lie. I know this is the perspective, but so is any other interpretation.

When I come home and someone is looking at me with tears brimming, begging for an answer to where I've been that isn't "with someone else," what are they asking? Tell me the truth? No!

It is an emphatic "tell me a lie!" So I had a couple too many beers to drive, got a taxi with a friend and left my phone in it. I'd have called from his, but he doesn't have your number. It's an ad-hoc picture constructed in response to your directions.

I'm still great. Your hopes have not been dashed against the truth, and the price of all this is simply that you feel inferior to me for a while.

Regarding lying, it is a bit of both. That said I once handed in an essay on how secrets are a kind of lie, so maybe I'm not the best person to ask.

If people run around saying, "what can I get for my money?" and someone replies "your hopes and dreams," what do they expect? Hopes and dreams. This is what they get.

Nobody promised to make them actually come true. That's why they're hopes and dreams, rather than expectations and goals.

Dianne
Can you give me some examples of what you mean by someone asking you to lie?

Fred

Perhaps we have just met and are lying in bed. There's something you want to talk about, you hope I understand and do not take offence, but you have been hurt before. Be honest; can you trust me? I look at you seriously and say, "of course; you can – you already do."

Then I laugh; you hit me and ask but no, seriously. I try to look honestly thoughtful for a moment and tell you that trust is not something you should allow others to allocate for you; it is much too much power to give others over yourself.

I just told you the truth; you turned it into a lie and later shall blame me for it. I highlighted the fact just asking was too little, too late.

I told you never to allow others to decide whether you trust them or not. I pointed out that you should be careful how you word things if they matter to you.

People lie to themselves and then demand I wear a yellow armband or have "doesn't painstakingly re-adjust the neuroses of every woman he meets before allowing them to be attracted to him" branded on my face.

Nevertheless, in another sense yes, it is true. You call it lying. I call it understanding how words work. Like at school, where they teach all sorts of simplifications in science class because they're easier to understand. That may be, but that doesn't make them true.

Then later you are taught something nearer the truth – something more consistently useful – and you have a greater understanding of and mastery of the subject than you did when you were working with the instructive lie.

If the student were capable of understanding the more accurate model, there would be no need to lie to them and no benefit in doing so.

Dianne
How do you model your "normal" behavior to create your mask? From others? As I mentioned earlier I am interested simply because it is a way of thinking or expressing that I am not accustomed to.

To me it is like watching a foreign movie and trying to learn the customs and language. Bad example but you probably get what I am saying.

Fred
Watching a movie to try to learn the customs of the society it depicts is not a bad example at all; it is a superb one. It's basically how I feel about a lot of things.

It's like I said to an ex: her boss laughed like she'd learned it from watching YouTube clips and reading, without ever having experienced humor or understanding how it feels.

She was a weird one, though. Scared me a little because I could never tell if she'd re-enter the room swinging a fire axe in some violent bid to find out where in a person, the funniness is kept.

Is that the sort of stuff you meant? It's hard to think of specific examples because to be perfectly honest most of my life has been spent in complete ignorance of the fact it isn't necessarily ordinary behavior.

I think once you understand the principle of being 'aggressively sure' of yourself, wielding certitude like a steel joist or battering ram, it's clearer. It isn't even unfair, because the other person is just as capable of doing it themselves.

If they care about winning the argument that much, why do they not respond in kind? Why are they letting someone else tell them what to think and trusting them beyond themselves?

Dianne
I have a much different story and history with psychopaths than members at my forum. The public in general has this disturbing view of what a psychopath is and how it translates into our daily lives.

I think there are a lot more psychopaths than anyone is willing to admit or acknowledge.

There is this distinct impression that if you look up the word, you will see a picture of Ted Bundy. Then in other cases the word gets tossed around so it has lost some meaning on the other end of the spectrum.

Fred

I quite agree that the terminology is unhelpfully fudged by popular conception. Psychopathic behavior does not need to constitute remorseless killers, but nor should it be applied to mean "manipulative, emotionally withdrawn male-typical behavior."

In some cases, there can be an element of denial that leads to the only explanation for someone having made a series of very stupid decisions is that they were manipulated by some sort of emotional vampire.

In others, there is a readiness to dismiss significantly psychopathic personality traits with things, like "he just knows what he wants" or "she's a very driven woman."

I could say to the people on your forum "I am what you hate, and I find it unfortunate that you have suffered as a consequence of people like me" and they would be howling for my blood. For looking bored. For not spending my entire life, every single second, reflecting for them to the exclusion of my own needs?

There are 'normal' (if you interpreted that as a sneer, in this context you are correct) people who do far, far worse than I do.

But they do it because they're sad. Really, really sad. I'm sorry officer; I have left these children without parents because I cried so much that bullets came out. Really? Oh alright then. 20 years with good behavior and we'll rehabilitate the ever-feeling shit out of you.

Because it was done for a reason, you could understand you would forgive a real monster who did something big far more quickly than me. Because, mostly, of things you do to yourselves.

The message? "Yes. We are 'bad'. That only means anything to you. You cannot take away our righteousness with your weakness, your fear, or you're passive-aggressive pawing." That is beautiful, don't you think? This idea. This joyous damnation.

I'm only making the best of a bad situation.

I try to prop the story up for others, but they can't keep up. When they drop out, what am I to do? Stop Running? Give myself up to them? They would not do it for me.

By most people's understanding, I will go to hell. As I said; damnation without hope of redemption. In my case, for basically nothing at all. So I fight for all I have. What matters to me. I do not apologize for that. Should the mother?

She could walk away and come back to have something left. I cannot. If I cannot have whatever love 'really' is, then I shall find my own, in anger. Learn to enjoy anger.

I was thinking: the problem with sociopaths is not as simple as that there are some. It is more that there are some but not everyone is one. If all people were, then I suspect some sort of second-order trust, and morality would have to be established for just the same reasons as the everyday versions appeared.

Maybe that's what emotions are; an evolutionary trait that helps individuals make decisions in accordance with the socially Freudeficial meta-ethical framework that has been established as an acceptable means of dispute resolution/prevention.

Since these things can't be justified any more than "bishops move diagonally" can be, irrational motivators that encouraged compliance would be strongly advantageous tools of social evolution.

So the problem really is that which underpins everything; an inequality in power balance, an innate unfairness in the way the world is structured. As if there needed to be more of those.

Dianne
Are people afraid of you? Should I be afraid of you? Should the "victims" on my website be afraid of you?

Bill
You can relax; none of them are appealing targets for me. I prefer my puppets in close proximity.

Fred
I have never raised my hand to a woman, have only occasionally been unfaithful, etc. - but certainly some things that would only be seen by others as at least very callous.

I do not think any of my friends are afraid of me. For me, yes, as I can sometimes (okay; often) show a reckless/impulsive streak several miles wide. Not always outright self-destruction, but not always not that either.

You don't need to actually imagine how it would feel, just be aware that it would suck, and therefore, it isn't a great thing to do to someone.

Aside from the cruel-to-be-kind instances that crop up occasionally, of course. I hate those because whichever way you look at it, you lose.

What I can tell you is that I have been told I can be terrifying. Not scary. Terrifying. What a thing to tell a guy with issues of his own! Do I think you would put yourself at risk? I would hope not. But do you not understand? People do. Time and time again. Sometimes it is the thing they want to do more than anything else.

I would bet there are people on your forum who are like that, who would be out of the door like a shot with the gentlest of beckoning. Others will seek people similar to whomever it was they're pining after, because it isn't the person, they want, but the treatment. The experience. The ideation. To belong.

And all the while I am showing you who I am. Look at those words. Think about them. Do they seem familiar? When do I do that, again? It's okay, because it is (hopefully) well-established by now what this is.

I have told you I warn people, and they plough right on through regardless. It is safe to watch from beyond the barriers, but it is chaos inside them. Literally, perhaps.

It's fine to like me, to talk to me. It is probably not so fine to get close though. Don't feed the lions.

Dianne
I am not sure why you have brought this up. I assure you I don't stick my arms into the lions' cage, let alone their mouths. Most of the people who write on my forum feel that they have been victimized. Do you think they are right?

Steve
Rereading some of your forum I kind of feel like a muse. I understand the mindset of the people on your forum and am not offended.

Dianne
I can see how you would feel like a muse. Keep in mind that people posting at my forum are in a very negative space when they show up.

Fred
I would like to share my observations about a few comments made by members of your forum:

"Brokengirl" needs to understand that she doesn't still love him. She just doesn't want to accept that she was wrong to do so in the past and that nothing is going to change that.

He doesn't love her. He says he does, but she thinks it is a ruse. This is because she doesn't really love him anymore and therefore, even the reflections look wrong now. She doesn't want to have been wrong.

Doesn't want to burn the photographs of her holiday in heaven, even though she has long since seen behind the scenes and discovered it was a sham.

Tell her to visit her parents, stay with them for at least a few days when they are around a lot and tell them what has happened. And all her friends. Or the cause of death on that one will be "choked on own pride." She needs to swallow it, tell them and stop being isolated.

I suppose the way we do it is by de-socializing our victims, breaking the links. I do not know if she will though, because she is already using his words.

Watch:

"Friends and family will be devastated if they heard he had got back in contact with me" (translation: you don't want to upset your family, don't let your weakness drag them down like it does everyone else around you, stay isolated.

Stop listening to him, start listening to them. This means stopping listening to herself for a while, because she's clearly not capable of acting even vaguely competently on the matter.

Either that or you're a feeble wreck in all areas of your life and always have been, leading to family and friends being sick of your constant shit and the inevitability with which you make bad choices.

If that's the case, the phrase "you've made your bed, and now you must sleep in it" springs to mind)

"I'm still confused" (translation: he tells me I'm confused a lot. If he destroyed her life, and it has left her in tatters. What is there to be confused about? She doesn't think she's confused really. You don't go into therapy for traumas you might want to go through again)

"I still love him for some strange reason" (translation: he keeps acting cocky and telling me he knows I still want him. It doesn't match up with what I know to be true, but he is still in my head, and therefore, I trust him more than my own senses, feelings and recollections).

Something else she has wrong: it didn't go wrong when he called her. It went wrong when she answered.

"Freebird" does not have trust issues with men. "Freebird" has trust issues because her own judgment wasn't enough to save her the last time. She needs to stop externalizing this and accept that she could make another mistake, and it could hurt her.

Nothing is guaranteed in life; she could be squashed by a rock from space at any moment or suffers a stroke or embolism or a million other things that could kill or cripple her. Does she let those stop her living?

Is her home devoid of electrical appliances in case one malfunctions and starts a fire or does she just try not to get the toaster in the sink while she's washing up?

Dianne
I like your thoughts on Brokengirl and Freebird and agree with them. One thing that happens, in my opinion, if people don't heal themselves is they will attract the same type but different hair color so to speak.

My goal is to acknowledge their pain, which is clear from their writing about their experience, and hope by reading that others are in the same position will give them more comfort and hope for the future.

I don't know enough about any situation to tell people what to do.

I am not sure people really pinpoint that they have been gaslighted, even when they have some distance from the situation. I think it pretty much goes undetected.

I can see how your answers would also push them to think it was more them than anything you had possibly done.

You seem to be good at making them feel like they are the problem and not yourself.

Fred
The whole point of the answers is to make it seem that way, so I agree. I assumed that people would give it thought over time and look back on it with a clearer understanding. If that's not the case, perhaps I do not understand people as well as I thought.

Many people say that psychopaths tend to resurface in their lives years down the line. This is true. However, so is the reverse; victims sometimes (often) exhibit a sort of addiction behavior.

Maybe I can save him! It could be different this time! Even if such a thing were possible, such thinking misunderstands the situation.

Dianne
I am not surprised by your comment. I think that people have the wrong impression, just because we are different doesn't mean we don't share some thoughts. Even if it isn't true, it is a nice gesture even so. That is my hope and has always been that they are safe and found the answers to the questions they were seeking.

Bill
I've read your forum (psychopath-research), at least most of it. I'm perplexed that some of your members call themselves victims. From what I've read, granted it's only a narrow view of the situation; it seems they were lying in wait to be taken advantage of.

Even the gazelle in the Serengeti knows there are predators at every turn. Do you think when one is taken by a lion the others are dumbstruck "Oh my, I had no idea there were animals that would eat me." Absolutely not. So why must humans seem so astounded when they have been taken advantage of?

Why is this surprising? I find it further fascinating that after being "victimized," they continue to call the person "My Psychopath." They have yet to remove this person from their inner self.

They remain a victim long after the psychopath has left and still use the possessive when discussing them.

Their vulnerabilities make them even more susceptible to another attack.

Dianne
I am not sure even I can answer your question why people are so surprised when they are taken advantage of. I used to watch the TV show called American Greed[18], and it just amazed me how people

---

[18] "American Greed" is a weekly American "true crime" television documentary series aired on CNBC. The program focuses on the stories behind some of the biggest corporate and white collar crimes in recent U.S. history; examples include WorldCom, HealthSouth and Tyco International. In addition, stories about common financial crimes that affect scores of everyday citizens (Ponzi schemes, real estate and other investment frauds; bank robbery, identity theft, medical fraud, embezzlement, insurance fraud, murder-for-hire, art theft, credit card fraud and money laundering) are also featured.

would mortgage their home to invest in some scheme.

There are a lot of dynamics at play, the person pulling off the scheme dangles things in front of them, makes them feel like only "special" people can join. They see the con's fancy cars and dream of having those things themselves.

And the main component is that it takes a kind and caring person who will paint any red flags white and get drawn down that path.

One thing is all psychopaths seem to lure in their victims and or explain their actions by appearing to be the victim in any situation.

People always feel sorry for the victim – just an observation. I think it is just human nature to feel for the "little guy" or victim. However, it is worded.

Bill

I too have watched American Greed. My surprise is not that people bought into the scam. Where I am surprised is when the victims are shocked that it happened to them.

Everyone knows I exist. Everyone knows what I am capable of. Why wouldn't I do it to them? What is surprising about this?

Dianne
I think that is an overstatement. I don't have any research but from many years of hearing from victims, I am not sure the entire world knows you exist.

Many times they just don't put a name to it. For example, when Bernie Madoff's[19] Ponzi scheme collapsed, it shocked tons of people who were well educated.

If they knew that psychopaths were roaming around them, I don't think that would be the case (being shocked when they realize they have been robbed).

That is the reason I am interested in this subject so more people can confirm their hunches about people they might suspect being a psychopath and for those others to learn that you do exist.

The problem as we discussed earlier is people only seem to sit up and pay attention to your existence when some major murders take place. And even then every news report has different ways they describe the person who does these things, some call the person a sociopath, some a psychopath and some narcissistic.

---

[19] Bernie Madoff was the former non-executive chairman of the NASDAQ stock market, and the convicted operator of a Ponzi scheme that is considered to be the largest financial fraud in U.S. history.

And then to top it off in one conversation a person will refer to all three of the terms, psychopath, sociopath and narcissistic, to describe the same person.

Bill

As I've mentioned before, my sanctification is not because others suffer. I would believe, as a psychopath, their suffering has little to no effect on me anyway.

My satisfaction comes from the power over others. While money is a strong motivator for me, a position of power is more appealing. This is true in my interactions with people.

I would much prefer to control you than take your money.

The reason being, if I take your money, you're likely to soon realize the cause of financial misfortunes, and I would be forced to move on.

If I control you, I can use you for a much longer period of time and eventually, if necessary, have you take the blame for whatever troubles may come my direction.

There are instances where I take nothing from my victim at all. In fact, this is often the case. They are most often simple pawns in a chess game.

The victim card is an ace in the hole. Your empathy is your weakness. In your haze of empathy for my plight, you will believe whatever I have to tell you.

This leaves open a door I can't help but to walk through. I will often set up my own mini "disasters" so that I can play victim in order to sway you to my cause. It's a simple math equation. A disaster that's not my fault + poor pitiful me = welcome to the puppet show.

Dianne
Are there some specific things you look for, the way they look or how do you look for character weaknesses and are these specific things you use when targeting them? As a simple example and I am sure you have much better examples.

For example, if you know someone has a drinking problem do you get them out drinking to see what they will say while drunk or do you use this to spread information and exaggerate what they are like and how it would tie into their performance at work?

Bill
I am especially good at intuitively knowing a person's character weaknesses and exploiting them. A psychopath, on the other hand, will display a character that isn't his (or less commonly, hers). Leading you to believe in weaknesses that aren't there.

Identifying this person early would provide me with a distinct advantage. Leading you to believe in weaknesses that aren't there. It is difficult to describe exactly how I look for character weaknesses.

I suppose it is partly instinctual. In a matter of seconds after meeting someone, I have a good "feel" for the amount of effort it would take to make them the newest addition to my puppet collection.

I keep a sort of mental list of everyone and their strengths and weaknesses.

If I know person A is prone to anger when challenged, he is a tool to be used when I need to create a confrontation. If person B is amiable and desires everyone to get along, they are tool to come to my defense if I'm challenged. If person C is prone to telling secrets when intoxicated, guess who is my new bar buddy. If person D can't keep a secret, they are my tool for the rumor mill and likely will become a patsy. So on and so on.

If you are responsive to flattery, then you're the most beautiful person I've ever seen. If you like to be glorified, I've never seen a stronger leader.

Every weakness will serve a purpose. Some are more difficult to manage than others.

I determine your weaknesses from the way you talk and respond. The words you choose to use, the way you present yourself, body language and other visual cues.

A short conversation will give me a good idea of your emotional and character makeup, exposing your flaws, weaknesses and more importantly, parts of your character that could be problematic for me.

When two people meet, they get a feeling about the other person, this is their first impression. This is not so with me. I don't get a feeling for you; I read you. Your interactions with me are like a How-To Manual.

I would much prefer to work with an emotional person. They would be much easier to control and much more predictable.

Fred
It seems to me the same difference as between pieces and player. If we imagine a world setting for a game of chess, with pieces representing their traditional military concepts, 'normal' people are the pieces. To them, they are charging over the top or defending the king from cavalry charges.

They know what it is like for things to be as they're described, not how they actually are. Compared to this, my feelings seem more like that of the player; problem-solving my way to victory.

As to how this manifests itself; it can depend. Ideally, it should be a very clear 'win/lose' situation, where I'm a great guy who went beyond the call of duty, and they are a pitiful, ungrateful, selfish disgrace. However, it's often enough to know that they'll be there again when I need them.

This is a different kind of win: I reeled you in, tossed you out and, just to prove that even forewarning won't help, reel you back in only to drop you at the last moment.

To show I can do it again. That there is no point in not going along with it, it will be easier on everyone to just go with the flow. I ask. And maybe to reinforce to myself that I'm really that good.

If the descriptions of psychopathic self-view are remotely accurate, I can only assume that this would be a strong motivator. I just see it as me being me.

Even after all the bullshit, I'm still more desirable than other guys. Not out of spite, often. It just comes naturally. You know how, when you leave the house for a meeting or something, you may check all your pockets/bags on the way out the door to make sure everything is where it should be, in case you need it? Like that. Muscle memory, but learned for a purpose rather than being some mindless twitch.

It can also work out well for both parties, if there is some way of coming away looking even better by the other person coming out of it well. However, when it comes down to their needing to be a loser – as it so often does – then yes, I can see they are the loser.

That's the point, isn't it? If I couldn't see it, I would not know I was the winner and would therefore, still be hard at work.

I am sometimes surprised by what people are upset by. As well as what they are not upset by, in a way.

Dianne
When you get some time, can you reflect on what people have said in the past?

Has anyone ever called you a psychopath after a heated argument? If so, I assume it was a girlfriend/lover?

Fred
I have been called all sorts of awful, horrible things by girlfriends. It doesn't matter how calm and reasonable I am. They rarely are. I have tried replacing calmness with shouting in turn, but when I shout, women tend to instantly burst into tears. Which is weird when you think about it. That said, I don't recall specifics from arguments.

Actually, I think unless you put me in a position where I'd need the information, I don't know whether I can remember what they were about.

They're always really the same thing, which is her going "I'm a needy idiot who wants you to give me my dream life, but only if you give it to me in my dream way."

I'm starting to think that the last 'proper' ex - the one I really, really hate - may have been really severe BPD. She wielded weakness like a knife, and I think was always puzzled when I failed to flinch or bleed when she used it. More grabbed it, twisted it and watched the guilt at what she was doing mount up.

She really deserved much worse than she got.

If I see her again, I intend to finish the job and leave her in no doubt who is in control. Urgh. She makes me feel sick. The worst of the worst.

Have you seen the movie *The Matrix*?[20] In that, it is said that the machines tried to create a utopia for people, but the human mind recoiled at something it considered too good. That is what actually happens.

All I ever get is sniveling ingratitude.

Dianne
I am interested in your relationship, and I hope by discussing it; we can show these things in a more accurate lens from your perspective, if you are willing to go there.

There is so much information out there in terms of victim stories etc., and frankly, none of it really comes from your view of things.

There are always both sides to every story. What do you think about emotional connections, for example?

What do you mean by this comment you made: "She really deserved much worse than she got. If I see her again, I intend to finish the job and leave her in no doubt who is in control. Urgh. She makes me feel sick. The worst of the worst."

She sounds like a pretty tough one, what made her the worst one?

---

[20] *The Matrix* is a 1999 movie starring Keanu Reeves as a computer hacker who learns from mysterious rebels about the true nature of his reality and his role in the war against its controllers.

Fred

I've decided that things have to come to an end with my current girlfriend. She's starting to annoy me greatly. Don't worry; I shall let her do it kindly.

Truth be told, I've concluded that any relationship with the girl in question would also be a relationship with her mother. Her mother is a very unpleasant, ignorant, fake person and I feel I am being brought more problems than it is really fair to expect me to handle.

My jokingly suggesting her mother's address and phone number be distributed in certain magazines, and phone booths was rejected. Her mom doesn't know how not to fight dirty, so asking me to clean up that mess without getting at least a bit of muck on me is stupid.

Six months ago, I was God himself. Now I am withdrawn and disinterested. In a week, a month, I shall be "that bastard."

Or did you mean the last live-with relationship? Because that was the girl who flew into a wall. She was so far beyond pathetic that the vicarious embarrassment of sharing a species with her is so great that even I can feel it.

She has a messiah complex like you wouldn't believe, and I say that as someone who, pretty much by definition, probably has one himself. But for her, 'victim' isn't a word to describe people. It is her name. Her badge.

If she were a Platonic Forum, she would be that of victim hood. She actually behaves a lot like I do in many ways, but she does it in a fucking OCEAN of fear and self-pity.

She was impossibly annoying and really quite stupid, but convinced she was a genius. No-one has ever been more wrong about anything. I had to explain prime numbers to her. She was a teacher.

The only time I have ever wished for the bus I am on to crash was when I sat next to her at the start of a two-week holiday. I say 'holiday' but I mean, like absolutely everything else in her life, 'extended therapy session'.

She had a hysterical fit because she said somewhere that was north of us was east of us.

Since I don't expect perfect geographical knowledge of the entire world, this wasn't a problem. I said (I think exactly) "Babe; we've doubled back since the last stop, so it is north now" and she absolutely lost her mind. On the bus from the airport.

We hadn't even got to the hotel, and she was already having an infantile tantrum - between telling me all of the faults she could list - over being wrong about something. Something she refused to accept, even when we stopped next to one of those huge roadside tourist maps. You Are Here! And... Oh look! Its north of us!

The fact that I was right was just further proof of how I was an unreasonable bastard.

Which when you look at it is textbook stuff. Total narcissism. But definitely not a sociopath. Just the most contemptibly worthless person to have ever walked the Earth.

Anyway, it all ended with me tearing her to shreds at the altar, in the holy of holies, beating her in her home stadium so brilliantly that I kind of feel happy with the outcome.

I agreed to couple's therapy and obliterated the only place she felt really safe, ruined her last delusion, so she could finally recognize herself as deranged and maybe go on to find reality and peace.

I have seen her once since then, and we were both all smiles and well-wishes. If she is stupid enough to cross my path again, I shall make her lack of father seem like a drop in the ocean when it comes to things she wishes hadn't happened to her.

Everything happens to her. She is pure emotion. Sadness and fear, pretty much through and through.

Sorry to break the crayons out again, but that relationship was a war-zone, and if I end up having to revisit it, then I shall not be taking any prisoners.

The 'last straw', I think, was her sister having a baby. She told me she resented me because we did not have one already. I told her we did not have one already because she was as far from convincing me she would be a competent parent as it was possible for anyone to be.

She went to stay with them to see the kid for the first time and expected me to take an entire week's holiday to go with her. Since I'd have been meeting it in about a month anyway, I said she should go on her own.

She came back, looked at me and said something, like "I want a baby, or it is over" and I said, "Okay then" and went out for a drink. We'd had a couple of counseling sessions by that point, and I think there were only 3 more to go, so I agreed we should finish them for closure.

According to the counselor, I am the most well-adjusted, patient and respectful man she has ever had as a customer. I obviously understood my girlfriend's issues, had gone above and beyond in terms of trying to help her with them, and it was understandable that perhaps she needed some time on her own to figure out how to resolve them without damaging those around her.

I am polite, insightful, charming, supportive, resilient, engaging and a great listener. I remain calm and controlled under pressure.

Obviously, this was all very gratifying to hear, but it wasn't getting to the nuts and bolts of the matter. Fighting back tears I explained that I may not have got everything right, but that true love does not seek to control.

Therefore, if the only chance of her having happiness was for me to lose her, I would take that pain. Because I was strong enough to do that for another person.

In other words, I was all the things that she wanted to be. In a very real way, she did it to herself.

Dianne
To be clear I have never thought that a psychopath would prefer to be anything other than what they are.

The sense of arrogance for lack of a better word and the thinking they are the smartest and most clever person in the room would certainly prove they are quite happy with what they are. Nothing wrong with that we should all be happy with what we are because that is just what it is.

I hope you can trust me enough to understand that I am only expressing my views.

Fred
One thing you should learn about me is "you can trust me 100%" is something I have said myself too many times to believe it when I hear it from others. It is suspicious. I'm not saying I'm suspicious now, but the trust issues go each way.

I was trying to get at this before; it is the move to make when someone needs to be reassured, to stop worrying. Why would they need to be those things? This is a very deep rabbit hole; I fear. Maybe bottomless.

My failure to conform would highlight the faux-grief of many others there and then the sham falls apart. People don't get their fix. You don't take away a junkie's needle if you want them to react well towards you.

You don't loudly sigh with boredom at a funeral. You probably don't feel bored at a funeral. I do. Exceptionally so.

They're like bad parties where you're only there because you know the host, and he's off somewhere else failing to entertain you. And I suppose I may sometimes forget myself without realizing.

There have been many occasions where people have been looking at me oddly for reasons unclear to me.

Again, that's not necessarily on my mind at the time. It is just the way things end up going. As always though, sometimes it is. Definitely more so if I've decided I am sick of someone, and it's time to make them end the relationship for me.

This is an example of the kindness thing I mentioned. I've given them the choice. They are making a decision they want to make.

I know they want to make it, because I want them to want it. Even if I didn't, any sane person would want to make it. However, they get the best side of the deal. Psychologically, it is much better to leave than be left.

If I just walked out, they would probably do something really stupid and messy. Alternatively, worse, decide they want payback. They don't want to want payback. It won't work.

Not because I don't care, although there's that as well, at least much of the time. Even so, it won't work because I know how they think and how they think I think.

If I plan far enough ahead – rare, admittedly – then I can even make sure this payback is beneficial to me.

One of them ran off and got with some lump of a bloke a few weeks after we split up. I wanted a bit of a break from her incessant shit, but she was banging the baby drum pretty loudly, and I knew she'd not wait. Best get out and then turn up like the world's most perfect potential father after a couple of months.

She thought it would hurt me if she moved on quickly. Instead, it just fitted neatly into the recent rumors about her being out of control and bouncing from man to man and this being a part of why ever-patient little ol' me had got fed up and finally left. She used to be engaged to a friend of mine, so he was most understanding on this point.

When reports got back to me that she was acting out and in denial, it was time for a reversal. Besides, I wanted to move back to that area for a bit. Finally, a rose with a note – some slushy poetry I'd bashed together.

It's all just nonsense, so try to say as little as possible so people will fill it with profundity – resulted in her meeting me for a chat. In the middle of her day at work. Behind her new guy's back.

I think it was three days later I was in the house again.

As she went to bed, I went to get the spare bedding for the sofa. She said to sleep upstairs. I said we wouldn't be having sex, because I was here to prove myself. I even said, "If we have sex tonight, I know you are going to wish we hadn't" or something along those lines. I got my things moved back in the following week.

And I was right, because she did wish, we hadn't.

I remember feeling nothing when an at-the-time-girlfriend had a serious accident, being hurled head-first into a wall at speed, other than annoyance that I'd waste my Saturday in an ambulance and hospital with her.

I really, really hated her by that point anyway, but was trying to 'win her back' after a break of a few months.

The whole accident happened so suddenly - she was a competent rider, if absolutely nothing else - that it caught me by surprise, but thankfully my - in retrospect - completely unsuitable reaction was seen as me being good in a crisis and cool as a cucumber. Which I suppose, in a sense, is true.

Interestingly, there seems to be a kind of simulacrum for grief for me.

This is because I absolutely hate losing. Cannot stand it.

I will re-establish previously happily trashed relationships at great effort, if I later decide I somehow may have been seen to have 'lost'. I am currently content in that I don't believe this is the case in any sense that I care about. If I do believe it to be, 'content' is no longer in my vocabulary.

All words are replaced with 'war' until the situation is resolved. Otherwise, extreme discomfort similar to severe boredom.

I'm already a magnet for bullshit and lunatics as it is. I don't need more problems. I need more fun. How do you deal with a sociopath? Be careful what you imprint on him.

Look at me as a loving boyfriend and I will be a loving boyfriend. Accuse me of being cold and distant, and I shall be cold and distant.

That is the only way the silly relationship games seem to work anyway. I've seen guys - really decent guys - been made out as turds because the girl they picked suddenly started seeing them that way. They did everything they could to fix things (well, everything they thought they could do) and ended up out on their ear anyway.

Because when it's a duck, it's a duck, and until you stop looking at it as a duck, you will never see it is also a rabbit. But if they'd responded properly, the argument would have been brief but the relationship would have survived.

Both would have what they wanted. And if she still thought he was being a jerk but didn't leave him; it only seems reasonable that what she wants in a partner is a jerk. Otherwise, why convince both, herself and him that he is one and then not end the relationship?

Not so much a thread on it per se, but the collection of advice and coping strategies I've read. "It's not me; it's him." Hey! That's just what I – he – was thinking! It is you. Like a coming of age, where they finally get it through their thick heads that they need to apply the rules for themselves.

After years of my standing there flapping my wings and gesturing towards the open sky, they finally leave the nest. And I've won. They're more like me for the rest of their lives, now.

Once all the crying finally stops and the unimaginably simple advice "get up and on with your life, be whoever you want to be and don't take shit from anyone because they'll take you for a ride if you let them" is at last understood. No longer looking at the words. Not even at the page.

I don't know how much fun it would be with an overly developed sense of guilt or if the sort of stuff, people say in the heat of the moment meant anything to you, though. I'd not considered that.

Feeling bad about feeling good? Ouch. Is this why people get so hysterical towards the end of a relationship?

Soooooo many women think 'psychopath' means 'male'. Always on the verge of collapse because by god does Princess Prissy have a lot of delicate sensibilities. "Heeeee shouted at meeeeeeeee!" *stamps foot*. Yeah?

Well don't be so pathetic then. Shout back. Stand up for yourself. I mean, obviously don't stand up for yourself. That would be tantamount to suicide.

That's a challenge. Just quietly leave, change your number and stop expecting other people to be strong for you. Don't be the kind of person who gets shouted at, if it is such a pressing issue for you.

I am honestly at a loss as to why people get so unbelievably agitated and jittery about shouting.

Dianne
Don't you ever get upset by other people's behavior?

Fred
Of course, I have feelings. Anger, for instance. Frustrating. But also what I have grown up to call happy, concerned, etc. That sort of how the masks work. I'm not totally devoid of emotion; I just don't really put much stock in it.

As I understand it, I should be 'concerned' I haven't heard from my girlfriend for a few days. Concern being "feeling ill due to curiosity over someone's failure to act normally," right?

I'm not, though. A bit angry, yes. Like she's just trying to suck more attention out of me. However, she can, for sure. Frustrated that she won't either stop acting like a fucking fool or leave. Actually, I just phoned her, because I am angry. If I did this to her, she loses her mind completely over it. I'd be called a jerk.

But my failure to constantly phone her when she does it to me - my failure to be like her - is also reason to call me a jerk. I do it, my fault. She does it, my fault. She was out for a 'meal with a friend' just after finishing work.

Did I just feel jealous? Tell me: if I came into your house and just helped myself to your things, would you be jealous or angry? Of course, I'm not 'jealous'. But there is a feeling that goes with the experience, none the less.

Anger at being stolen from. Anger at having to protect my territory. At this point, I don't really know whether she's worth the effort. I really don't like people trying to play games in relationships.

Put it this way. If she told me, she'd been raped on her way home from a bar; my instinct would be to tell her how stupid she was for being in the situation. People put themselves in such and then expect others to pick up the pieces.

Because I don't fall apart at the first hint, the world isn't made out of candy floss and kittens; they usually look to me to do the picking. I wouldn't shout, of course. I know that is Not Done.

Someone who loves me committing suicide would look pretty bad, wouldn't it? So I wouldn't shout, but wait a couple of days until they pulled themselves together a bit. Then I'd gently suggest that maybe going to bars isn't such a great idea if they don't feel up it.

Ah, she called back to apologize. I gave her the Floating OK. Oooh... live demo? An example, just for you. A show home. I can't show you round, of course, but we can look at it from the outside and marvel.

Sure, I'm full of bunnies and remorse for a life mis-lived. Just a misunderstood lost soul, really. Will you take me under your wing and make me whole again?

Dianne
While getting people to sleep with can be a natural part of growing up, what kinds of things did you do to make sure you achieved the end goal? Did you ever have steady girlfriends?

Bill
I did have a steady girlfriend throughout school. We never slept together. She was a "good Christian girl" and really increased my reputation as a respectable guy.

The people (I say people because I slept with both guys and girls) I slept with were usually from other schools. I often chose people older than myself, students from the community college or sometimes young adults.

The manipulation was mostly with guys. I had a thing for getting a straight guy; it was the ultimate prize for me. What worked most often was to invite over a beautiful girl and have a few drinks.

Once she has been drinking I would talk her into calling a guy I wanted, and to invite him over. This is where it was tricky. I needed her to drink enough to pass out but not before the guy arrived and started drinking.

Once the three of us started fooling around, I would quietly suggest to the girl how tired she looked, or that she didn't look like she was feeling well.

The power of suggestion often convinced her to go sleep, or call a friend to pick her up. This left me and the now intoxicated straight guy alone and worked up.

All I had to do was talk a lot and fast, be convincing and understanding, and he would be up for the new experience. It was reliable and when successful was not only a fun night, but the guy knew I now had damaging information.

I am married. Interestingly enough, I have my suspicion about my spouse's potential psychopathy while at a lower degree than myself.

Dianne
Did you know your wife for a long time before getting married? It seems curious to me that she shares your personality type yet you are unable to be conclusive in your observations of her?

Bill
As far as my wife, I would bet that she is not a full-blown psychopath. She certainly has some tendencies. She is very self-aggrandizing, and I would say the parasitic lifestyle fits her. At times, she can be emotional, but she certainly isn't emotionally needy.

She has a conscience, although, I would say it is below average. She is empathetic, to certain people in her life. We moved in together two weeks after dating. Lived together for three years before marrying.

I make significantly more money than she does, but recently she has increased her annual income significantly. The marriage has lasted, and I would say well, because we both use each other.

We are open to bringing in other people for sexual encounters, allowing us to satisfy our sexual fantasies/desires. She is typically submissive, which works for me.

Dianne
Would you say that you prefer male and male sex or primarily with females, or it just doesn't matter? Does your wife have a preference on who gets invited into your bedroom?

Which one of you does the picking and what is that process? Do you have regulars who join you or different extra partners each time?

Bill
Sex is sex really. Depends on my mood, whether I prefer a male or female. Sex with a man is more physically empowering to me. Sex with a woman is more of an emotional control. We usually choose together; we have similar taste in guys.

I have the final say. Typically, we only invite someone once. It prevents them from becoming attached to either my wife or I, which would not end well for the third party.

That is drama that would not go well for me, should it ever become public.

Dianne
Some of the people on my forum refer to relationships with psychopaths as "skim and discard," meaning a shallow relationship that ends with the psychopath discarding them without caring.

Is this true for your relationships?

Fred
I see people on your forum talking about this skim and discard behavior. That they really cared, really wanted to know 'him'. But that he never knew them.

This is gross ignorance and an enormous lie. Yes, he did. It was they who skimmed. If they had not, they would have known what they were dealing with. Had he not read them thoroughly, cover-to-cover, twice, he could never have learned them. Actually, no.

That's not quite right. He didn't read it. They read it to him, even the words that are just words and don't really mean anything at all. His crime was to listen. Theirs was not to stop talking. But listen to the hate. The rage.

He is singing about love the only way he knows. What love means to him. What it means to me. What it means, really. Just very few people will ever take an honest look and those who do are reviled, cast out before they infect anyone decent. Too late.

One day, if I live long enough, I will be normal. Without changing a single thing about myself. Perhaps I shall have my redemption after all.

Besides, being liked for being someone else means nobody actually likes you. This can grow to be a problem in relationships. Trust me.

I have an analogy. I like analogy and metaphor in general. Not least because they're basically my only way to make sense of many things, you all seem to do intuitively. Anyway, here it is. I'm proud of it, because it has a lot of truths to it:

The object of my romantic attentions feels the same way as a canvas does about the attentions of a great artist.

I think that line is an expression of the underlying structures I've been discussing regarding capitalism or at least our current interpretation of it.

There must be losers for there to be winners. Society has made these targets so significant that they impact the way people think, leading to the idea that "destroying" someone is okay in order to gain advantage in order to X.

In this case make money, but the point is the same because it is of setting aside the interpersonal element and saying, "this is what we have to do and these things (emotional sensibilities) should be no obstacle to that."

Is it a typically sociopathic view? Probably. But it's also an example of what I mean when I say I am not the one with the disconnect.

Dianne
Does this mean that you think it is the victim's fault if they are abused by a psychopath?

On the television show, "American Greed," people would mortgage their homes to invest in some worthless scheme. Was this their fault, or the one who tempted them?

Fred
Narrative grammar; it ends the way it begins. White knight turns up to save the day and has to sacrifice himself nobly in the name of a higher cause. Nobody ever remembers all the murdering he does between the "arrives to save the day" and the grand heroic gesture at the end.

Probably, because they call it "saving the day" to salve their precious consciences and keep their idiotic fairytale world nailed together.

If people spent more time trying to understand how stories worked rather than just chanting the same-old ones, it'd be less difficult for them to make sense of.

Whatever frothing insanity she would have come out with, my advice to her now would be the same as then: get down off your crucifix and move on with your life, get psychiatric help and for the love of god don't breed.

Dianne
You are right, escaping one terrible situation doesn't mean that is the end of dreadful situations. What happens many times is another person with a different look takes the place.

That is why sometimes people will be married to one alcoholic or disordered person and hook up with another one but maybe the hair color and profession are different.

The basic package with all the things they think they are escaping is really what in the end they might be most comfortable with.

Fred
I think the problem may be that most people want to reach out, just for a tiny touch. A quick glimpse. The thrill of putting their hand through the bars while the lion is on the other side of the enclosure. But most people also can't let go.

Not because I'm so wonderful, although maybe I am. They can't let go because their stupid emotional responses go "oh look, a connection! Intimacy!" because if I were most other people, it would be.

I would similarly be drawn like a moth and make connections that held me in place. I don't though, and then it's hooks-fluff-rrrrrip because what else can I do, carry you around forever? They expect intimacy.

When people press a button and don't get the response they expect, they usually press it again. And again. And again. And by the time it's clear there's nothing forthcoming, the machine has eaten all your money, and you're thirstier than ever.

If you are so sad, you kill someone - self included - then you are an idiot. All you are doing is moving the sadness about to people who will, sooner or later, want to shift it back to you. The problem doesn't go away; it just keeps piling up.

You are making a clearly sub-optimal decision because instead of solving the problem that you claim you're concerned with - whatever made you sad enough to open fire, I guess - you're instead solving the problem of "god damn I really feel like killing these jerks because my emotions rule me and make me do really, really dumb stuff".

But not having the emotions is a bigger transgression than murder.

People say they think they value X or Y, but they don't. They value I. But if I were open and honest about myself, I'd be 10 times more likely to be wrongly imprisoned for murder than Captain Sadface would be, even after he'd been released. He's 'fixable', after all. A fixed scum bag is preferable to a well-functioning outsider. Better the devil you know than the devil himself.

Is that it? I'm an unknown, and that means the same thing as the devil. I've been called it before. Satan, a demon, all sorts of childish nonsense, designed to hurt. To make themselves feel better by comparison. Here's a big circle.

Everyone inside it is good; everyone outside it is bad. They all do the same things, but that's what the words mean. Similar = good, different = bad. And if the cover is ever blown, here come the exorcists, and it is no more Fred.

No crimes, lots to contribute, but he's different so let's pump him so full of drugs that he may as well be dead and then stick him in a cell to rot.

It's a shitty way to treat anyone, but at least they wait to see if normal people will actually do anything wrong before they're punished for it.

This whole stupid dance goes on and on and on. It is of your creating. Everyone bought into it, cared for it, and after it was so obviously dead, they curated it. Like a museum. It is not my fault the exhibits aren't very interesting.

Look at it this way; if you know someone is hyper-competitive, and you are not, why would you compete with them? If you know someone is happy with confrontation, but that it really upsets you, why would you provoke confrontation and then whine about being upset?

If you know the lion can bite your arm off in the blink of an eye, why put your arm through the bars in the first place?

If their personal ship is sinking through their own stupidity, unreasonableness or greed, you do not blame the rock they dashed themselves to bits on. It is a rock. It cannot help being a rock, and it didn't go about being a rock with any degree of malice.

You can steer clear of it or approach it in a suitable way, but just ploughing through oblivious to the dangers is nearly always how people do it to themselves.

Why would I leave an obviously unpleasant person unadjusted, living happily in ignorance of their own gross failings? It'd be like littering or walking past a rape without intervening.

When I see ugliness, I want to correct it. When I see beauty, I will take a dim view of any who tries to pollute it for their own ends, intentionally or otherwise.

Maybe that's what I am; part of society's immune system, a way to excise the rotten tissue, clean the wound and let it heal back to something healthier.

Who is the worse man; the one who really cares but walks out in a tantrum while his wife sobs on the floor, or the one who stays, holds her, soothes her and goes through ALL of it with her? Hot tears on a supportive shoulder.

Every racking sob caught and collected, echoing through a strong chest. Hair stroked; head held steady with a tender hand that pulls you into safety. Don't you see the beauty? Because it is there. Very much so.

It is what is says: a painting of the strong protecting the weak, even from themselves.

What does sadness feel like? Salty and hot and shuddering. Pitiful. Overflowing with pity for oneself to such an extent it is hard to contain. And it happens in your arms; it washes over you, and you heal the wounded, scared creature and make them whole again. More than whole.

I mean, when something breaks, you might as well make some on-the-fly improvements.

Less hysterical, less likely to pick a fight they are destined to lose. Making better decisions. Stronger. Moving nearer to thinking clearly and independently.

At least, I'm there to help pick up the pieces. Mr. Sadface isn't. He's too busy being sad. I'd be hated less if I just looked at them like garbage, called them a worthless bitch and walked out never to return? Like hell I would.

My failure to abandon people to failure and collapse is sociopathic. People want unrealistic perfect. If they didn't, I wouldn't exist.

Dianne
Like everything else, where there is pain, there is money. I have followed a couple of groups that claim to "heal" kids who have these issues. Really, it is more about grabbing the parent's money and getting paid to tell them that if they follow their advice, everything will work out just fine.

Like paying to have delusional thinking. It is like some of these cancer "treatment" centers who prey on people by claiming they can cure you.

Some things you just can't cure away. It is really about playing on desperate needs. One online group where I read for quite a while is mainly populated by foster parents and grandparents.

They lay the blame on the parents for abandoning the child. I don't know what good that does, blaming others can only get one so far.

Fred
You described exactly what I have said about neediness, and the lies' people want to be told. Rather than confront the fact that it is meaningless, that it just happened, and it won't change and there is no blame to assign; they pay witch doctors for magical rituals. Do you know why?

It is not because they are good people, although they may also be that. They are not paying for their child's sake. They are paying for their own.

So they know they 'did the right thing' and/or in the hope that they'll convince themselves, they've brought home some magic beans. Which they will then never, ever try to plant.

Everyone knows that magic beans stop working when you plant them. They just turn back into regular beans. But it's okay, because they didn't plant them, so they still have the potential of planting them if they so choose. When the time is right. Which they never do. Because it never is.

It would shatter the glass, and the reflection would splinter.

Dianne
Then what would you tell these people who want to change?

Fred
Either live in fear and never achieve anything or accept that you might have your head knocked off by a meteorite at any moment without anything you can do about it.

If you wait for assured success, you will never succeed because you will never take any of the uncertain opportunities that are ALL life will give you.

That's as good as it gets. Accept it and live an imperfect life. Anything else is having a tantrum because the world does not rearrange itself to your whims and will only ever leave you with an even less perfect life than that which you've turned down.

The difficulty here is that my instinctive reaction is "don't be so over-emotional," "grow up" or "don't be so stupid." All any advice boils down to is, "make better decisions," which usually translates to "learn how to make better decisions."

The best way to do that is stop lying to yourself and accept that there are things you want but cannot have. Either because they are unobtainable, or because they are imaginary.

In other words: stop telling yourself who you wish you were and start doing things to be it. If you want to be rich, find ways to earn money. If you want to be informed, learn things.

If you want to be creative, create things. All these things take hours and hours of practice and work. Why expect anything different in your personal life? Stop expecting Prince Charming to do all the work for you, for the perfect relationship to land in your lap.

Address your expectations and be honest with yourself why people don't like you in the ways you want them to like you.

Do you want to be liked or do you want to be yourself? If you want to be liked, then by definition, you will have to allow other people to dictate how, what and who you are. Obviously, I would see only the latter answer to even be worth considering.

There are billions of people on this planet. Somewhere there have to be some that will like the real person, so it is win-win really. I mean plenty of people like me, and I'm a soulless monster right out of nightmares. You guys should be swimming in friends without having to compromise anything about yourselves at all.

Dianne
Do you actually like anyone?

Fred

There are a few people whose company I can tolerate for extended periods of time, and I do not wish to lose any of them. I particularly like when people who are very smart talk about themselves, it beats hearing from average people any day of the week.

Considering I see stupidity as something akin to a mortal sin, it is important to remember that it is something I will feel the need to comment on.

To assert superiority? Maybe. But from my perspective, I just really, really despise stupidity as it is intellectual ugliness; tantamount to an evil in itself.

You could say that I get as angry about the stupidity as I do about the immorality, but I am painfully aware of both. In a very literal sense.

I have a perfectionist streak and when something is going well only to be derailed by outside influences, I can become quite frustrated. By 'outside influences', I generally mean the stupidity and intellectual cowardice of other people.

I face my demons every day, and it makes me really angry when other people refuse to do the same.

I also get immensely pissed off by people who apparently don't know what the word 'compromise' means. Com-promise; a promise that is not dependent on the actions of just a single individual.

People throw the word around like they're accredited experts, then they spend months moving the goalposts ever nearer to themselves before taking even a single step towards the line of compromise themselves.

At every step, it is "can you meet my halfway on this?" with only one person taking a step so many times that eventually 'halfway' is 'agree with my original demands completely'.

That's no way to conduct a respectful relationship, and if I ever catch people doing it, that is usually the same time as things start getting messy.

I will go to war to teach them not to try to take advantage of me like that, to try to paint me as the bad guy because they are too stupid and self-centered to give an inch themselves or even admit that is what they are doing.

Don't ever play chicken with me because if I've decided that I'm not backing down, I won't. Hitting a problem head-on and with full commitment, even if it means self-destruction, is something I seem to be much more willing to do than most people. But then so is just turning around and walking away without a second thought.

I do not know how anyone can look themselves in the mirror and consider themselves a rational being if they can say, "the toilet roll is on the holder the wrong way around." As if there is a 'right' way to align paper that's about to meet an ignominious end, if you'll excuse the pun.

Yet not only are there people who think this, but they never stop to examine why they think it or whether being upset by the 'wrong' alignment is in the slightest bit sane. If it isn't, they don't think what might cause it and how it can be addressed.

Which is because people make rules for themselves and cling to them in order to feel there is some order and sense to existence. I'd say looking at the evidence honestly; I can only conclude that there is little to none of either.

A person's ideas about what they think is important are often very, very severely out of whack with what their actions indicate they think.

You can claim to care for the poor all you want, but if your actions are to cut out their welfare and paint them as scroungers, then it's pretty obvious the words don't mean anything other, than "I know these are the right noises to make for approval."

Good dog, have a biscuit. That's most people. It really, really is.

I dislike hypocrisy intensely and highlighting examples of this to people is something I feel is almost a moral obligation. Okay, okay: and enjoy doing, sometimes greatly. But not indiscriminately or only out of self-gratification.

I do also think that much of society is irrational, hypocritical and morally ignorant to a quite painful degree, so with the bar set accordingly low I may even be able to pass for a decent human being, not merely a human being.

Dianne
I can see that in your sense, you are telling them what they are setting up for you to say. Kind of like when someone asks, "This skirt doesn't make me look plump, does it?" Well, gee, let me guess what the answer to that one is.

You just told me you were thinking you look fat, and I know enough about people to know better than to agree with you, so the "does it?" part at the end gives me the clue to say, "Of course not; you look great."

Fred
The "does this skirt make me look fat?" question is an excellent working example. The answer to that varies:

(Early, fun) – Cock my head and squint. "Hmmm... I duuuunnnnooo." Wait for the start of response and big playful grin. "Don't worry; if it gets to be a problem, then I'll start drinking heavily!"

(Early, getting serious) – "Babe, if anything, you make the skirt look fat. We might need a security detail for this."

(Nearing the end of the whirlwind phase) – "Sure. It makes you look Chinese, too." Said very matter of factly, but with a flashed grin.

(Breakdowns begin) – "Not look fat..." and a deadpan look. Then, just as there's about to be a response, just a twinkle of the eyes.

(The endless chaos) – "No. That's the cakes. What do you want me to say?" Then walk out of the room in a way that drips with the feeling you're much too busy to spend time stitching together the various dependencies and desperate bids for validation of a naïve idiot.

An aside: I was just talking to a friend of mine. As this is more at the forefront of my mind, I thought "why do I like him?" The answer is, I think; he is what it feels like to be a good person. He doesn't really care either, but he does it from the opposite corner from me.

He doesn't care about the fact, there's loads of shit in the world; he just gets on with being a good person because that is what he wants to see in the mirror. He has told me as much. That's a damned sight more clever than most normal people ever manage.

I can't say I understand why he puts himself through the grinder constantly, but I respect that he's understood how things really are. Even if he doesn't realize that he has understood it. Be who you want to see in the mirror and never look away.

It is entirely possible that I am capable of lying to myself when required. However, I strongly believe that I am intelligent and rational enough to spot any glaring inconsistencies and, if this is the case, it is only likely to be very mildly so.

It is partly due to this than reading some of the accounts of behavior on the forum was instructive; does it ring true to me at all? Yes? Interesting.

Dianne
I have never had a weight problem and while I would never agree with someone saying they are fat I often hear things like; you are so thin you make me sick, and then they laugh.

I guess we have some things that people feel it is okay to be critical and be passed off as a joke. Passive-aggressive behavior is a trait I am not too fond of.

Fred
Passive-aggressive behavior tends to make me freeze.

It's like being viciously mauled by a goldfish. Taunted by infants. You think you're clever with words, do you? You think you can manipulate social norms and situations to get away with things?

Even thinking about it frustrates me. NO! The little smiley or breezy smile is a drawing on the fridge. It is allowed to exist there and only there. It isn't there because you've done well; it is there because I'm tolerating it out of convenience.

It is better than having to sort you out from an incoherent emotional implosion. A whole lot more dignified for you, too.

But passive aggression is a really very big, red flag to wave at me. It's saying, "Show me how it's really done". Only it won't be always be passive about it.

If I come downstairs in the morning with a hangover, and you ask me cheerily how my day is going (because I got in at 5am soaking wet, freezing cold and outrageously drunk, mumbling innocent confusion as you moved to the floor for the rest of the night), the answer to that is about to become 'vindictively'. Passive aggression? Pfft. "About as well as the money-sink you call therapy is."

"Downhill since I found you didn't die in the night." Get a long stare of disbelief and then left alone for a snooze. There is no charm to these. They cannot be interpreted as a joke. And they gnaw at your brain.

They're just a standalone comment - as you can imagine, they don't foster a conversational atmosphere - to which no normal person has a response. What, you hope my family dies? You're not going to say that! I'm clearly not going to give a shit even if you do, so all you'd be doing is making you hate yourself more for crossing that line.

So it sits there, a paper cut on your day. By evening, you'll be fuming. Raging. Too much anger for you to know what to do with, which generally means what you end up doing, is crying.

Like that's some sort of proactive step to improving your situation. Oh how proud I feel, how impressed by your independence. That'll stop me being a jerk, for sure.

Or it might be a friendly, life-is-grim-for-us-all humor, as if I haven't noticed the tone. After all, if you know you're likely to be met with accusations of infertility and lectures on the fortuity of such for the future of unborn children in general, you're not going to say anything in the first place.

But they do and they get increasingly agitated, ever more clumsily sarcastic and eventually sort of start hiccupping, in an attempt to not break down sobbing or grab something heavy and try to cave my head in like Bambi on crack.

Chest shakes, voice wavers; tears start and stop; they fan themselves with their hands and then, usually while trying to busy past on some theatrical errand or other, slowly sink to the nearest flat surface and just lose it.

This might be a seat, but it also might just be the middle of the kitchen floor.

There is something fascinating about it, actually. A sort of gravity from the intensity of experience. And a... it isn't protective, but... possessiveness? Authorship.

They want a beautiful life. They always want a beautiful life. But you can't make an omelet without breaking eggs.

Do you want your dream story or not? Then let me write it and stop complaining about the scene-setting and character development. Never, ever gratitude.

Remember, this can happen without any input from me. In fact, it is more likely to happen the less input I give. I've been what is always asked for in someone you're disagreeing with; calm, reasonable and giving thought to solutions.

I think from this you can safely assume it is fair to say that I do not like passive-aggressive behavior either.

Dianne
How could you ever have a real relationship with anyone, with this attitude towards other people?

Fred
I want a relationship. I know you're going to tell me I shouldn't have one. I know that broadly speaking, in social terms, you're right. But I still want one. I know it will cause damage, no matter how hard I try.

Do I live without love? Waste away and try to be a good person in all the ways I think are stupid and weak? Other people might tell you they don't get lonely. That's a lie.

I can ignore close friends for a decade and then explain it away. That's easy. Being me, on my own, knowing that not only is the person I'm with going to get hurt, but that any connection will only ever be a lie, what can I do?

Is the reality that if I love, I will annihilate? Can I do the former without the latter? Do I prefer the latter to the former and have just been lying to myself all these years?

I was not arguing, merely explaining and expressing my frustration at an inability to convey my meaning adequately. As I said, it is quite common. That only causes it to be more frustrating, rather than less. Perhaps it is why I am more comfortably expressive when engaging with a more poetic, metaphorical approach.

The sad reality is probably more along the lines that very few people if any will understand what I'm trying to get at. Not because I'm smarter, just because there's a terminal disconnect between my experience of the world and their own experience of it.

Perhaps my anger is just sadness kept at extreme pressures. Frustration at the disappointment of once again being denied the depth of communication and connection I subconsciously crave.

Oh poor little old me, so misunderstood. Self-awareness is as dangerous a tool as it is a powerful one. It certainly doesn't bring happiness, although neither does it create unhappiness.

A broken bulb does not bring darkness to a room; it merely fails to bring illumination. *Nos tacemus* [21].

Dianne
Do you ever need help from someone else?

---

[21] This means, "We are silent." It is taken from an ancient Latin poem about the nightingale, in which the last line is *"illa cantat; nos tacemus; quando ver venit meum?"* [She sings; we are silent; when will my springtime come?]

Fred

Most people would give me no help. None. I had out advice like pamphlets, and I'm taking advantage, simply because I am more capable. This is damnation. Even though I've never really hurt anyone.

Well, maybe a couple of fights when I was young and didn't realize how fragile bodies are. Nothing worse than the odd broken bone though and it was when I was very young.

Violence attracts attention and makes the fun parts of life more difficult to get on with. However, otherwise, I don't steal, am not violent... nothing 'big'.

I just leave a trail of emotional destruction behind me, mostly by accident. Yet damnation it is. Even if I'd never caused so much as a tear, the fact I could is reason enough to cast me out. And so I was.

Look how that worked out. Society subconsciously punished a thought crime. Could further socialization have 'cured' me? Doubtful, but possible I suppose. It can't have hurt though.

The problem is, I think, that normal people would find being cast out very difficult to come back from. They see it as both punishment and confinement.

I saw it as more like being given an objective view of how things really worked (as opposed how people had described them as working) and where all the unlocked doors and open windows were.

Nevertheless, if the choice is damnation or the sort of feckless insanity that most people call life, I think I've probably gotten the better side of the deal. Of course.

It strikes me, reading that back that perhaps that's why people hate it so much. Their choices are my choices. I do not take away freedom so much as show it for what it is. A puppet show. I show how similar we are, if you wipe away the make-up and change out of the costumes. I am a reflection of you.

You are a reflection of everyone and everything you've ever seen, heard or thought. It's a muddle which I clear up for you, so you can see the real you. Alternatively, the you that you want to be real.

I hold your hand while the layers are peeled back, and you see how little choice, there is for any of us. That there is no deepness to anyone, just confusion. Fleeting patterns in chaos.

And sometimes I'm so caught up in the act that I don't even realize I'm doing it.

I'm quite pissed off that I've spent much of my life trying to be good and never quite understanding why it doesn't go right. It's because what I mean by 'fix' is rarely if ever what the other person means by it.

Hence the current attempt at self-discovery, I suppose. Is it even possible? If it is, is it worth it? There's only one way to find out.

I think I can see why past events have upset others better, understanding my behavior under this light. But am I just a joyous wrecking ball? Am I incapable of resisting the temptations people offer?

If I'm very honest with myself, I think this is probably still about control. Power. Games. But maybe more expert ones, more subtle and synthetic, better sustainable with less risk.

Eco-psychopathy, if you will. Maybe it's a generational thing, but there are many very rational arguments propounding living sustainable as advantageous.

Don't drain resources, but balance the load. I am interested in systems and interactions. The more complex the system, the more refined the interaction, the more elegant an achievement it is. Let me translate that for you: the more glorious the victory.

Dianne
You have said that some women are attracted to psychopaths. Why do you think some women who have been victimized by a psychopath go on and marry someone just like him?

Fred
I think everyone is that in need of finding something to complete them. In an ever-changing world, as a dynamic perspective, they think there's a lasting fix.

Maybe the only difference is that when the short term fixes stop working, I am freer to move on because I never expected it to last. Once the good of the situation is consumed, move on to a new one.

You don't spend all your time listlessly pining over one particular meal, do you? You don't only ever listen to one song or album, endlessly on repeat.

What most people do with relationships is akin to eating progressively slower as the amount of food on their plate diminishes. Then they cry when all that's left is sprouts and gristle, how they will never enjoy another meal again. Yes, you will. Grow up.

Make love? A fatuous phrase, but one dripping with the kind of syrupy implications that don't connect to anything real. Just words to make 'fucking' sound less like it is. Less animal.

Society has warped people into some sort of puritanical shame state. Sex is fun and potentially inexpensive.

The world is often not fun and very expensive. I don't understand why people don't treat it more like alcohol or food. They're programmed to be prudish.

What those people do – the married ones – is not just find someone similar. They try the whole thing again from scratch, getting with their ex as he was when they first got together.

After a long, traumatic relationship and breakup, what better than someone young, charming, passionate and fun. Because, my dear, that was exactly the same reasoning as got you into said relationship in the first place.

What the lion did not consume, the hyenas shall take.

That is why people herd, is it not? Safety in numbers, stay in the center and don't slow down. We evolved that way, as a species. Not like bison or fish, but to an extent still. Packs, not herds. Same principle but applied to predators who pack more punch per member.

If I'm under attack, and I know I've got an allied wolf between me and the threat, I may consider the threat dealt with. I would not feel the same about being separated from the threat by a single fish, however.

And so the herd runs on. But why? We don't have any natural predators anymore. Are we waiting for evolution to give us the OK to stop? No. The truth is, you run.

You run because of people like me. At some point, parts of the herd started preying on one another.

What greater evolutionary advantage than looking like your prey, being protected by them? What hogwash.

The truth is people run because people run. I've nothing to do with it; I just sneak into narratives like that and assume an important position.

CHAPTER SIX

Psychopaths and Work

*Those who fear what they should not fear, and
who do not fear what they should fear...
go the downward path*
—*The Dhammapada, The Path of Perfection*

Dianne
What kind of work do you do; would you consider yourself successful?

Steve
I am a lot of things in a work way I'm a chef, driver, maintenance man, painter, mine operator, gardener, laborer, blacksmith. I tend to get bored with jobs the same as partners, but I tend to have success at all I turn my hand to.

I have a focus that most lack and use it to learn as much as I can about my task as long as the money's there that is. I don't work for free.

Dianne
In an earlier statement you made when I asked whether you preferred the term psychopath or sociopath, you said you preferred no term at all because the stigma would be detrimental to your goals.

What are your goals? To fit in better in society or how would you describe them? Without being specific are you more on the white collar side of business and successful

in terms of financial gains and position or do things get in your way?

Bill
My goals are simple. I want whatever I can get. Currently, I'm finding the most success by moving up at my current place of employment. I work for a government agency.

Moving up in this government agency allows for a higher social status, greater income, and a more public face. This in turn increases my trustworthiness.

Dianne
Our corporate structures seem often to be headed up by psychopaths. Who is better suited to extract exorbitant profits? They let the greedy shareholders hide behind them ignoring their depraved methods.

Fred
What you say about corporate structures is true. Not just those, but I think capitalism in general. Structure forces you to choose your actions from a limited set.

Money lets you distance yourself from consequences. I used to play rugby. It is all right to dive at someone and smash them to the ground on the rugby pitch. It is acceptable to stab someone in the back in the boardroom.

However, now the boardroom is everywhere, and the mask of civilization is slipping from normal people. Why? Because they've finally started catching on to what they're really afraid of; themselves. What is inside?

The drives, the urges, the 'nasty' thoughts, the private monologues and delusions of love, riches, and... I cannot help but smile. There should be a third thing, shouldn't there?

I know of love, because most people like nothing more than lengthily propounding their imagining of it. I know of riches, because I don't live deep in the void between stars and am in possession of senses.

What don't I know, Dianne? Can you tell me? Is there a third thing? If there is, I believe it to be a lie similar to the first. There is power over your environment.

People label it different things depending on which area of life; they're exercising it over or from which source they're drawing it, but that is all it is.

Dianne
Do you think the corporate structure accepts psychopaths? It seems they fill a role that others might not feel comfortable in.

Fred
Yes, corporate structure allows and seems to encourage psychopathic people in their ranks. I don't just mean it rewards psychopathic behavior, although it does that too.

I mean that society is reprogramming itself to be more like I am. In fact, I think it's reprogramming itself to be something a whole lot worse than I am.

I have tested this and I know it to be true, but think heavily on it because it can show you the future: if you break down in tears at work, people will worry you are going to sue them and cost them a lot of money.

You will be treated with suspicion. If you explode in disgusted rage, people will give you a lot of money so that you don't sue them. You will be treated with respect. Why? Angry people fight.

People who're crying won't even stop you taking money out of their pockets, if you upset them well enough.

It's just business. Nothing personal. You know how it is.

Dianne
From what I understand the main difference between us is the lack of a conscience; I call it the stuff that keeps people up at night.

For example, if I worked at a company and was told that I would have to get rid of a lot of the people, knowing they had children and family members that relied upon them,. this would cause me a great deal of stress.

It would be very hard or even impossible for me to do. However, from what I

understand from looking into how some psychopathic corporate people operate they can do the same tasks and be quite fine about it.

Fred
Business is sociopathic behavior taken from walky meat and put into big stone and glass temples. Business is a church to sociopathy.

That is all any church is; the embodiment and unquestioning pursuit of a given set of values. In past jobs, I have had almighty rows with managers over their stupid decisions on whatever it was, only to go for drinks with them that evening.

One person tells another person they are not getting some money they worked for because of Business Reasons and then they both carry on chatting about how incredibly awesome they think Breaking Bad is or what is playing on the radio.

Do you see what I mean when I say I feel somewhat singled out in all of this? Everyone does this all day, every day.

Africa starves; Asia is some sort of non-consensual orgy, and the Euro ends the day up 1.4 points against the Dollar.

I sometimes make people cry a bit more than someone else would have made them cry. Not even because I upset them more, just because they can't follow the strands to make sense of it all. Or, you know, just let it go and move on.

Dianne
If business is a church, what does it worship? Money?

Fred
Business worships the concept of consolidating strength and punishes sentimentality. Religion worship's god - who is really no more of making a bit of yourself that reflects back your hopes and soothes your anxieties - and punishes bumming.

Bit of a weird one to pick for the second part there, but the whole edifice of religion is pretty incoherent anyway so maybe that's to be expected.

I'm one of what I can only assume is a tiny minority of people who subscribes to neither of these belief systems as 'true'. Yet what am I criticized for? Doing business.

Nobody ever believes in a god who doesn't only want them to change in ways they already think they need to change themselves. Isn't that a coincidence?

I wonder if leaving a religion hurts as much as leaving a sociopath.

Dianne
How do you get along with other people at work?

Bill
It's a delicate balance. In order to move up certain actions have to be taken. Certain people stood in the way. They had to go but there could be no

suspicion that I removed them. So I manipulated those around me to take care of that for me.

Dianne
Do you use any gaslighting techniques to control people at work?

Fred
Since I don't really give a hoot about work, I find business as a concept fairly distasteful and couldn't care less if any given company burned to the ground overnight.

I probably have never felt the need to engage in that sort of stuff in that environment. Besides, who wants to work with confused, unstable, scared, angry people all day? I would see it as counter-productive to my already stretched tolerance of being at work in the first place.

Having said that, whenever I end up in a dispute with a company (utilities, phone, council, the entirety of India - you name it, I'll try to take it on single-handed if I'm pissed off enough), my approach may well be seen as gaslighting like it's going out of fashion.

I will muck companies about, move the goal-posts and generally try to force an error and make pursuing me such a nightmare that they'd rather just lose whatever money it is they want.

This is a kind of constant background to my life, and I enjoy it greatly.

I'm also somewhat notorious for it among friends and colleagues, with some of my emails doing the rounds to great acclaim.

It can vary from just total nonsense to confuse them, histrionic threats of suicide, intentionally vague legal posturing... anything at all that I can think of and whatever I feel like at the time, basically.

The point is if you make them say enough things, one of those things is going to be a wrong thing, and they'll have to back off or be taken to court themselves.

I will happily take on other people's disputes just for the pleasure of settling them with little effort but a lot of panache. I'm basically a one-man charity, thinking about it.

Bill
Recently, an employee had the nerve to confront me. This was done in a semi-public area of the office. The witnesses were close enough to know that something was happening but not close enough that they could hear every word.

I knew this employee was going to take this further and the truth could severely damage my long-term success in the agency.

Instinctively, I began to provoke this employee in order to increase her anger, as I knew she was prone to raise her voice and appear aggressive.

Once she began to raise her voice, at my provocation, I terminated her.

Being a government agency, we have a union and with that require a hearing after termination to ensure there was just cause. Knowing this, I began to "stack the deck."

I spoke to several key employees, who were present during the exchange. When I spoke to them, I was sure that I did not directly bring up the topic of the argument, but gently "guided" the conversation in that direction. When they bring it up, I interject key components to the story that they did not have.

I would supply information, such as; she cussed, made threats and had no basis for her concerns. By the time I was done, the witness believed they had actually seen the story that I provided them.

They gave firsthand accounts of the created reality I provided them.

Furthermore, during the interview I was certain to include that created reality into my statement. I also used truth to my side. By providing factual events, in a slightly different chronological order, my story was believable.

When they received the statement from the terminated employee, the facts she gave line up with mine but appeared in a different order than mine.

This gave credibility to my statement, since essentially the facts were the same. Since the witnesses collaborated my version of events, it was determined that the employee was intentionally not disclosing her threats and swearing.

The termination was upheld.

The ones that are most difficult to manage are what I call, the "amiables". They are the ones that want everyone to get along, sacrifice something they want to keep the peace, look for the option that is mutually agreeable.

These types are very easy to convince into anything.

You would think this would be a breeze, right? Absolutely not. I can convince them what I want them to believe, and tomorrow someone else has convinced them into something else.

They need constant attention. Constant reassurance.

They also experience heavy guilt when making the tougher decisions, such as terminating an employee. Which requires more work on my end and, once convinced,

I have to make sure they do not change their mind before it is completed. I will typically avoid them. I look at it as an investment.

What return will I get for my time? If I can get the same return, with someone else, for less time invested, I will choose someone else. Unfortunately, this is rarely an option.

If there is only the one person in the position I need to influence, then I have no other option. Most things he hears about me are who I may have stepped on or recently pissed off.

It's a common occurrence that I make someone angry. Luckily, I have the ability to turn this around on them, making it appear that they are angry that I called them out on their mistakes. This does create enemies from time to time, which must be dealt with.

I have a special person, who reports to me and is blindly on my side. When he hears anyone say anything negative, he makes sure I'm aware. He also explains my version of events. It's an automatic defense system.

The most effective, however, is when he tells me what the employees are saying regarding my changes to policy. This gives me the ability to prevent messy conflicts with the union by stacking the deck in my favor early on.

He also aids in convincing them that my ideas are actually better for them.

Dianne
When we discussed relationships, you described gaslighting as mirroring.

I am not so sure gaslighting is really mirroring in the sense that who would ask anyone to help them feel, angry, confused and all the feelings that fall-out from a person who is the one being gaslighted?

Your comment about why you don't do this at work was what got to me.

I guess you wouldn't want to be around people at work in that state but being in a

relationship with someone in that state is just so foreign to me that it is hard for me to grasp.

I can't imagine on any level doing that to anyone.

Can you please elaborate on this comment: "I think it would be fair to say I have an abiding hatred for avoidable imperfections. Maybe unavoidable ones, too."

Fred
For the comments I made about work and your response re: relationships, that's interesting. Maybe I see people's behavior in that sphere to be irrational and chaotic anyway (perhaps in the ways they see mine to be in other areas?

I couldn't say), so I'm just trying to fit in and hum along. I don't enjoy causing people suffering (weeeeell... very rarely.

It'd be too big a lie to say never at all, but it really is very, very occasional that I do), but I don't like them causing themselves suffering either.

Not least because that by definition and implication means they are causing me suffering, so sometimes adjustments need to be made. To help them.

I really am very well intended 99% of the time and not that rotten to the core the other 1%.

Dianne
Are you good at what you do at work?

Bill

A few years back, when I was a low-level employee approaching eligibility to promote to supervisor is when I first began a larger-scale manipulation. All the supervisory positions were filled and there was not much prospect of an opening in the near future.

As you can imagine, this was not acceptable to me and something had to be done.

As luck would have it, a supervisor, who I had already developed a "bond" became pregnant. I instantly saw this as an opportunity. I learned of her pregnancy from other channels, and she was unaware that I knew. I expressed my desire to promote, to demonstrate what a great employee I was wanting to pick up more responsibility. I also began to tell her that I was thinking of having children.

I expressed my concern over the hours I would have to work, and that I really wanted to be available to my kids. I quoted research, which I completely made up; that children with parents who work only part-time are much better adjusted as adults.

They need that constant contact with a parent. How difficult it must be to raise a child with two full time, career oriented parents. I explained how, in the end, it was good for me that there is no position open right now because it allows me time to develop and focus on my family.

I planted the seed. I knew she was now thinking of her own child and what would be best for her family. I know she was wondering if she could be a good mother and work full time.

She also knew I would be a good, trusted replacement if she decided to leave. Since, to her knowledge, I didn't yet want the position. She felt, from what I could gather that my advice could be trusted, as I had no other motive than her well-being.

I did some further manipulation with management and the union to plant the seed to create a part-time position. Once this brand new part time "assistant supervisor"position came open, my target supervisor jumped at the opportunity.

Of course, she stepped down from Supervisor to assistant supervisor and was now a part-time employee. This now created the vacancy I needed.

She has since regretted her decision, but since I have filled the position, she cannot go back. She now works for me, as well as a second part-time job.

Fred
Give me a complex system – a given economy, for example – and the way the company handles it. I then poke it a bit, find all the flaws everyone else hadn't seen because they didn't know how to look, rinse and repeat. I found that an entire team had exactly zero impact on figures, for example.

Connecting up sets of numbers in ways people hadn't thought of. Finding the relationships that no-one bothered to look for because they found the first one and settled for it. Pressing the buttons.

Finding out which ones do things and which ones aren't connected up, wasting control space.

I am currently away from my last job, and I don't want that job back. Not least because I recognize that one of the people above me in the company is far too similar to me and he can afford good lawyers.

It was time to move on anyway, but by going now I get a bit of free time on full pay and a bunch of money to not come back.

They messed up and they know it, but if I push him then it's going to get into a fight that I don't really want right now.

I've got a ton of shit on him though, so in a year or two the industry regulators are going to be very busy. It's kind of a shame, because not many places pay well for people to basically create problems for them.

Dianne
So, you are getting paid to stay home; that is nice, but perhaps what got them to pay you to stay home is another deal in itself.

I don't get the idea it has you moping around the house wringing your hands worried about getting your job back.

Fred

Why would I mope around the house for being paid to not work? I would be more likely to mope around the house because I have to go to work to get paid. Which I usually do, in fairness. Work can be fun.

Since then, I've moved across the country (for the relationship with the girl whom I now despise) and finally got myself a decent job. I'd been there 3.5 years.

During that time, I had a couple of failed relationships (both with good friends), a cancer scare (that I had to keep to myself); my parents split.

My dad had a stroke, and my company started having problems. Not financial ones, but structural ones. I had to move house to somewhere 50% more expensive (I think I've moved 12 times in the last 10 years and almost none of them by choice), and my earning capacity took a hit.

Stress started building up, and things got worse and worse. I was then off with stress for two weeks at the end of October, start of November. I came back to be treated like a criminal and was still promised many things to resolve the situation, none of which materialized.

Today I arranged a settlement agreement. I shall walk away with about $10,000 USD and a good reference, on good terms with the company. The alternative was them trying to fire me for gross misconduct for shouting at my manager that it doesn't take a year to fix a minor issue.

CHAPTER SEVEN
Eyes

*"The soul, fortunately, has an interpreter –
often an unconscious but still a faithful
interpreter - in the eye."*
— *Charlotte Brontë, Jane Eyre*

Dianne
Has anyone commented about your eyes and if so what were some of the comments? From what I understand and what I have observed, when the mask is off, the eyes change.

It is something that once you see it; you never forget, kind of like looking into a scary black well, and a feeling that evil is lurking.

Some think that the eye color changes but what really happens is the pupils become huge and black. You say it doesn't happen often, do you have examples of the types of things or events that have made your eyes change.

Steve
My eyes change color from green to blue to gray. They go gray when I'm mad at someone, and I have people tell me that I'm freaky scary when I am mad, and I stare at them like a robot that wants to kill them.

Fred
I do not know about blackness of the eyes, certainly in myself as I'm not often angry at a mirror. Maybe I should arrange some arguments in front of one to check. If people report seeing black, I can only speculate that this is because it's a color they associate with fear or emptiness.

What you are seeing is not black, but emotion. Or the gap where it should be. I don't know, since I don't know if we see people the same way.

I like to think I am good at understanding these things, but nobody ever proved anything with a single datum, so I could be wrong. It does seem that when it happens – the eye shine, that is – it will be noticed.

I've got a good stare. Maybe because I'm more of a fringe case. I don't get the black pits' thing. Maybe it's not what I am at all.

Or perhaps I am dead inside, but there's some sort of ghost of who I would have been, what I should have connected up with, where everything plugs in. I don't see that it matters, but it could be interesting to know.

Dianne
Do people tell you that they see the anger in your eyes? Or that the eyes don't connect with your smile?

Fred
When I'm angry, my eyes are very fierce, I'm told. I mean obviously, because I'm angry. But beyond that, they kind of light up, apparently. I can give a

good rant and was often complimented for monologues when I was still involved in theatre, usually on the grounds that "the feeling poured off of you" and "you said it with your eyes."

I've never had anyone comment that my smile doesn't match my eyes. I suppose it wouldn't be the sort of thing anyone is likely to say to my face anyway, so maybe that doesn't tell us much.

I am very good at maintaining my mask, though. It can be forgotten about for days, left securely in place. Only something truly unexpected and sudden is likely to so much as wobble it. And of course sometimes I may choose to remove it, for effect.

In case you didn't notice, I have a great sense for the dramatic. But show just enough that the question is raised in their mind. Then spend a while reminding them how wonderful I am.

I suppose, in effect; it encourages them to condition themselves: how could you think such a thing? There are you thinking that, while off goes Fred, giving puppies to orphans in his free time.

You wanted a puppy, remember? Why are you so resentful that these orphans now have some, then? Do you think you need one more than they do? Get off my back.

Stop assuming the worst in everyone, just because your dad left/died/hated you. Clearly, it is an absurd thought. A nasty one. Hurtful. Don't think it. You will, though. Next time the mask is dropped, for example. Is there something wrong with you?

Dianne
I don't know if it is anger or frustration that gets the mask to drop for lack of a better term. But there is an association that the gloves come off and the pupils get huge and black.

I think a less sophisticated, non-socialized type has a harder time controlling it or getting it back into check after it happens. It must be hard to be on guard but actually aren't most of us on guard most of the time.

Steve
People see emotions in people's eyes, but mine work like a mirror in the way people see what they want to see or what they are feeling. This also helps to control people because they think I feel the same, and that makes them nicer and have less of a guard up.

Bill
I am aware of the term "mask" and its intended meaning. This, however, is not exclusive to psychopaths. We all wear a mask of sorts depending on our environment.

Where the psychopath is different is that we wear a mask not to hide our flaws but to exploit yours. The person you need me to be in order to trust, confide in, support and promote is the person I will become.

Being free of unpredictable emotional reactions and guilt, I am free to be whatever, whenever and then change that when necessary.

Dianne
As far as the mask situation, I agree that everyone has them but yours are a different kind, and I am not sure we are on the same page in describing yours, which is the interesting part of this conversation.

Have you ever dropped your mask and then heard comment about your eyes appearing scary?

How would you describe these many masks? I doubt you believe in God but are one of them the image of good church going person or what in general are they as best you can describe them?

Bill
While the mask and act come instinctively, I certainly know that I am doing it. It takes energy to be convincing. So I imagine my mask most often slips if I am tired or angry. I usually am self-aware of this and take steps to seclude myself in my office or take a "business" trip somewhere.

The last thing I need is to lash out at a target before they have served their purpose. While this has happened before, I am usually quite good at making amends. It can also serve to prove my humanity.

Everyone is moody from time to time right? I suppose another instance when my mask slips is in situations where empathy is expected. This is a particularly difficult emotion to emulate.

Dianne
There is an old proverb that says, "The eyes are the window to the soul." What do you think about that?

Fred
I've always liked the phrase 'eyes are the window to the soul'. Sometimes the window to your soul looks back at you, across the table on a date or in the staff kitchen when you're getting a coffee.

Just a little signal that says, "let me show you how well I know the real you." It's attractive. Maybe you put on a dress and do your hair. I put on a context and smile.

You cannot see my soul through my eyes as I lack one (soul, not eye), you believe. Well, distance forbids even if you wanted to check, which I can't imagine you would. But there is a window in my words.

Dianne
As far as the soul, I don't think you have one as we know of them but haven't visited these thoughts in ages, so to be fair I will give it some more thought.

I am always willing to have my thoughts on subjects evolve. At first glance when you see into those dark black eyes, it is like you are looking into the pits of evil.

How this relates to a soul is a pretty big subject that I will have to take some time to think about.

I didn't have a name for those eyes until my first forum when people were talking about the shift in the eyes. It was then that I had the aha moment and clearly saw what the eyes of less extreme versus this extreme person looked like.

Some people on my forum have said they can see pure evil in a psychopath's eyes. That they were staring into the eyes of madness. . Here is how I see it.

I have been in the presence of a few people who were clearly psychopathic. If something bugs them, there is what I will call dropping of the mask, and the eyes turn to pure hatred and black.

It doesn't matter what color their eyes may be normally; many at my forum have also reported this happening.

It is an interesting transition from the situation. I think it is like how cops will say once they smell a dead body you never forget the smell.

Fred
Staring into the eyes of madness; at what point does introspection become waffle and self-referential nonsense?

As for windows into pure evil, I have some thoughts on this. I will repeat that I do not think I am evil. My actions would not be considered to be, for the most part, all that far from the norm. I do not set out to 'do bad'.

I think that what many people mean by 'evil' is similar to what they mean by 'madness'. Crazy people don't make much sense because they're not acting rationally.

But they're also obviously crazy, not empty, so people let them off. It's madness without the madness. Alien. Hard to process. Watch:

Maybe it doesn't make much difference, since without the eyes and faces it is only ever going to be reading through the script and following stage directions anyway.

Especially the words I have in mind, because they were completely subconscious and I have only just realized what they are doing.

Dianne
What do words have to do with eyes?

Fred
I can feel my eyes change as I write some comments, just as they would if I said them. Words are tools, but eyes and smile are weapons.

Having said that, of course I can do melty-eyes. Or wise. Or deep. Or regretful. Or lively. Whatever I want, really. There even seems to be a degree of connection between color and current performance.

My current partner seems to think my eyes are hazel. Others have said bright blue, greenish blue, violet, grey.

They really are very beautiful, my very best asset after my mind. I have had female friends ask for pictures of them. Quite 'sane' ones, even. I have been bordering on stalked by people – both men and women – who have been fascinated by them.

However, as mentioned, my eyes are very sympathetic. I mean that not only in that they can look full of sympathy, but that like many other things; they are what people bring to them.

For eyes, my pupils can become pretty huge at times. I have had that mentioned a few times, but thought you meant more a change to the tone of the iris. That does happen, too. Is the pupil thing not normal?

Surely, when you are most alert, you want to take in the most information, in order to make the best decisions. The world can be very clear and bright when you do that. I suppose it could just be what it feels like to have someone pay you complete attention.

Dianne
What other kinds of things do people say about your eyes?

Fred
In terms of eyes, I've had various comments. Here are some examples:

- They're amazing/beautiful/so intense (social and complimentary, but often not romantically inspired)

- I feel like you can see through my act (often nervous but hopeful, like a relief that the act doesn't work so can be dropped. Semi-romantic but often from people who have good reason to have an act up in the first place)

- I would not want to meet you in a dark alley (from guys, usually when I've ranted about something that has annoyed me greatly, such as someone behaving thoroughly unacceptably towards someone I care about or some great social injustice I've currently got a bee in my bonnet over)

- You looked at me with nothing but hate (after an argument with super-bitch ex)

- Are you even looking at me? (During arguments or other negative but highly emotionally charged moments)

- I feel helpless (from a few girls when things have transitioned from friendship/meeting to be physical/romantic, when I've looked right at them and said something they feel is insightful/passionate or whatever)

Those aren't word-for-word, but they give the sentiment clearly enough, clichéd as they are. I'm not sure how many people really look at other people, pay them their full attention and don't filter it through some sort of social pretense, but I suspect it isn't all that common.

The more intense and direct, the more likely there is to be a comment and the more emotive it will be. I've also been told lots of times "I could get lost in your eyes," usually said with a distinctive tone that is halfway between complimentary ("they are beautiful enough that I could get lost of them") and slightly concerned ("there is something about them that I want to figure out but can't").

I think what I have managed to do for the last couple of days have been look at me in the way that I subconsciously look at other people. I regret to say that I appear to be quite a complex problem. It has been tiring. Hah. Is this how it feels? Have finally worked it out, only to happen to myself?

Now that is an idea worth further consideration. I shall think about it. However, I will end this with a thought. If empathy is seeing things through another person's eyes, maybe in my case, I need to try seeing things through my own.

Reverse the flow, as it were. One end goes up; the other goes down. And vice versa. If I do it long enough, will I find a person in here somewhere?

Will I piece the bits of them back together if I look at how they all fit together hard enough? Could I make one? Like a mask that once you put it on you can never take off? It would have to be a really good one.

By which I mean: can I repair myself and if I cannot, I remake what I have into something static but better?

AFTERWORD

*"There is no index of character
so sure as the voice."*
-- Benjamin Disraeli, Tancred

I hope you found reading the transcripts of these interviews insightful. Distilling over 125,000 words of such varied conversations presented a challenge, but I believe these excerpts provide a very interesting glimpse into the minds of some ordinary psychopaths. I hope that through reading this, some people will realize that they exist all around us.

One of my beta readers, Gail asked me how writing the book made me feel. It seems only fair, having asked my subjects to express their emotional responses during the interviews, to end by sharing my own reaction.

I found the conversations both fascinating and horrifying.

One day, I was so creeped out that I actually put black duct tape over the camera on my computer. Steve was the most disturbing for me. The eyes on the cover are his.

We were discussing eyes, and without my asking, he sent me a photo of his. I was most horrified when he talked about giving medications to his victims. I actually let out a shriek that brought my dogs running into the room.

I found that they would begin by saying one thing, usually what they thought would be appropriate and make them look good, and then they would contradict it as they continued to write. They would lose track of themselves in the conversation. This was one reason I decided to correspond only via email, to get a sense of how they might respond in the spur of the moment. I also did not want them to have access to my emotions or responses.

Fred was the most interesting to me. Through most of our conversations, he was clearly on a manic high. I ended up with over 85 thousand words from him alone.

I still hear from him on occasion. He was introspective and curious about his own mental state. Fred had a caring mother who clearly must have known on some level what her son was, and she seems to have done a great deal to socialize him.

You can see Steve's disconnect, not understanding why and how his mother feels about him. I think they all had mothers who helped them.

Several times, when the conversation turned to someone's death, one of them would interject, 'It wasn't me.' I was never sure if he was being overly defensive, trying to hide something, or if he was actually innocent but feared I would assume it was his fault.

When I was talking to Fred about Steve drugging his victims, he could not simply say , 'that's abhorrent," and leave it at that, Rather, he had to keep going and expose his own aberrational thought process by explaining that he wouldn't do it. Not out of moral concern, but out of fear of being caught.

Sometimes, I would wonder, 'is he messing with me again?' Is he trying to make me think he's dangerous out of some misplaced sense of humor, or to gain control?

After reading some of Fred's dialogues, you might be tempted to think that psychopaths may have morals, emotions, and intense desires to engage in relationships with and relate to other people.

Be careful, because that is how they hook you. You never know if they are telling you the truth, or just what you want to hear.

Overall, I am glad that I made the decision never again to work for anyone else, particularly after interviewing Bill. I was upset about the way he described how he set that poor woman up by getting people to see only their interaction and his version.

No matter how much I might have wanted a promotion when I was working for a corporation, a machination like his would never have entered my mind.

Thanks to all that you that have read my book. I would be grateful for your comments and feedback. If you want further information or wish to leave a comment, you can visit my forum where I have set up a special section for conversation about my book.

If you are looking for a diagnosis, you can also contact me, and I will help guide you to the right specialist for your confidential requests.

I take confidentiality very seriously. I will be unable to answer any specific questions about the people I interviewed in this book, such as their location or contact information, but I would be glad to answer any general questions.

A special section of my forum is available for any questions or comments you might have, and confidentiality is preserved there as well. You will find it at www.psychopath-research.com.

Very Best Regards,

Dianne

FOR MY NEXT BOOK – I AM SEEKING PARENTS

I am working on my next book, in which I will interview parents of psychopaths. I am particularly interested in hearing from parents whose child is a suspected fledgling psychopath.

I plan to write about the experiences parents endure when they have a child with the types of behavior described in this book. Please contact me if you are willing to share your experiences, in confidence.

dianne@psychopath-research.com

REFERENCES

References for the Foreword

American Psychiatric Association (1952). *Diagnostic and statistical manual of mental disorders.* Washington, DC: Author.

American Psychiatric Association (1968). *Diagnostic and statistical manual of mental disorders (2nd ed.).* Washington, DC: Author.

American Psychiatric Association (1980). *Diagnostic and statistical manual of mental disorders (3rd ed.).* Washington, DC: Author.

American Psychiatric Association (2013). *Diagnostic and statistical manual of mental disorders (5th ed.).* Washington, DC: Author.

Birnbaum, K. (1914). *Die psychopathischen verbrecker.* Leipzig: Thieme.

Cleckley, H. (1941). *The mask of sanity.* St. Louis: Mosby.

Cleckley, H. (1976). *The mask of sanity, 5th edition.* St. Louis, MO: Mosby.

Gacono, C.B. (2000). *The clinical and forensic assessment of psychopathy: A practitioner's guide.* New Jersey: Lawrence Erlbaum Publishers.

Gacono, C.B. (2015) *The clinical and forensic assessment of psychopathy: a practitioner's guide* (2nd edition). New York: Routledge.

Gacono, C.B., Loving, J.L., & Bodholdt, R. (2001). The Rorschach and psychopathy: Toward a more accurate understanding of the research findings. *Journal of Personality Assessment, 77:1,* 16-38.

Gacono, C.B., & Meloy, J.R. (1994). *The Rorschach assessment of aggressive and psychopathic personalities.* Lawrence Erlbaum Publishers.

Gacono, C.B., Meloy, J.R., Sheppard, K., Speth, E., & Roske, A. (1995). A clinical investigation of malingering and psychopathy in hospitalized insanity acquittees. *Bulletin of American Academy of Psychiatry and the Law, 3,* 387-397.

Gacono, C.B., Meloy, J.R., Speth, E., & Roske, A. (1997). Above the law: Escapes from a maximum security forensic hospital and psychopathy. *Bulletin of the American Academy of Psychiatry and the Law, 25,* 1-4.

Hare, R D. (1991). *The Hare Psychopathy Checklist-Revised Manual.* Toronto: Multi-Health Systems.

Hare, R. D. (2003). *The Hare Psychopathy Checklist-Revised Manual.* Toronto: Multi-Health Systems.

Hart, S.D., Cox, D.N., & Hare, R.D. (1995). *Manual for the Psychopathy Checklist: Screening Version (PCL:SV)*. Toronto: Multi-Health Systems.

Heilbrun, K., et al., (1998). Inpatient and post-discharge aggression in mentally disordered offenders: The role of psychopathy. *Journal of Interpersonal Violence, 13*, 514-527.

Kraepelin, E. (1907). *Clinical psychiatry (A. R. Diefendorf, Trans.)*. New York: Macmillan.

Losel, F. (1998). Treatment and management of psychopathys. In D.J. Cooke, A.E. Forth, & R.D. Hare (Eds.), *Psychopathy: Theory, Research, and Implications for Society* (pp. 303-354). Dordrecht, Netherlands: Kluwer.

Lyon, D.R., & Ogloff, J.R. (2000). Legal and ethical issues in psychopathy assessment. In C.B. Gacono (Ed.), *The clinical and forensic assessment of psychopathy: A practitioner's guide*, (pp. 139-174). Mahwah, NJ: Lawrence Erlbaum Publishers.

Marcus, D.K., Lilienfeld, S.O., Edens, J.F., & Poythress, N.G. (2006). Is antisocial personality disorder continuous or categorical? A taxometric analysis. *Psychological Medicine, 36*, 1571-1581.

Mayer, J.D. (2005). A tale of two visions: Can a new view of personality help integrate psychology? *American Psychologist, 60*, 294-307.

Ogloff, J., Wong, S., & Greenwood, A. (1990). Treating criminal psychopaths in a therapeutic community program. *Behavioral Sciences and the Law, 8,* 181-190.

Pinel, P. (1806). *A treatise on insanity (D. Davis, Trans.).* New York: Hafner.

Rice, M.E., Harris, G.T., & Cormier, C.A. (1992). An evaluation of a maximum security therapeutic community for psychopaths and other mentally disordered offenders. *Law and Human Behavior, 16,* 399-412.

Robins, L.N. (1966). Deviant children grown up. Baltimore, MD: Williams & Wilkins.

References for the Introduction and Chapters

Hare, R. Multi-Health Systems. *PCL-R.* Retrieved from http://www.hare.org/scales/pclr.html

Lilienfeld, S.O. & Arkowitz, H. (2007). What "psychopath" means: It is not quite what you may think. *Scientific American.* Retrieved from http://www.scientificamerican.com/article/what-psychopath-means/?page=1

Rogers, T., Blackwood, N., Farnham, F., Pickup, G., Watts, M. (2008). Fitness to plead and competence to stand trial: A systematic review of the construct and its application.

Journal of Forensic Psychiatry and Psychology, 19, 576-596.

WebMD. *Bipolar disorder.* Retrieved from http://www.webmd.com/bipolar-disorder/mental-health-bipolar-disorder

Wikipedia (2015). For general definitions and information about people, words, scientific terms, movies and plays.

Resources

Psychopath Victim Support Forum
www.psychopath-research.com

Made in the USA
San Bernardino, CA
10 October 2015